Toys and Reasons

BY ERIK H. ERIKSON

Childhood and Society (1950, 1963)
Young Man Luther (1958)
Insight and Responsibility (1964)
Identity: Youth and Crisis (1968)
Gandhi's Truth (1969)
Dimensions of a New Identity (1974)
Life History and the Historical Moment (1975)
Toys and Reasons (1976)

The Child's Toys and the Old Man's Reasons
Are the Fruits of the Two Seasons.

—William Blake

ERIK H. ERIKSON

Toys and Reasons

Stages in the
Ritualization of Experience

W · W · NORTON & COMPANY · INC ·
New York

Copyright © 1977 by W. W. Norton & Company, Inc.
First Edition

Library of Congress Cataloging in Publication Data
Erikson, Erik Homburger, 1902–
  Toys and reasons.

(Godkin lectures; 1972)
"Based on the Godkin lectures . . . Harvard University in 1972 under
the title Play, vision, and deception."
Includes bibliographical references.
  1. Developmental psychology. 2. Play. 3. Reason. 4. Ritualization.
5. United States—Politics and government. I. Title. II. Erikson, Erik
Homburger, 1902–   Play, vision, and deception. III. Series: Godkin
lectures, Harvard University; 1972.
BF713.E74 1977 153   76-18851
ISBN 0-393-01123-2

for Joan

Contents

10   Contents

Preface

THIS BOOK is based on the Godkin Lectures which I gave at Harvard University in 1972 under the title "Play, Vision, and Deception." The Godkin Lectures are under the auspices of the John F. Kennedy School of Government, and are expected to apply themselves to some aspect of "the essentials of free government." At that time, a rather improbable theme had struck me as elemental, namely, the relationship of childhood play to political imagination.[1] But I would not have had the courage to enlarge on this subject had it not been for the fact that the Godkin lectureship that year included a seminar attended by a university-wide group of faculty members and students who were selected on the basis of ongoing work that seemed to meet my approach halfway. For the theme of my lectures is by its very nature most elusive in its varied manifestations, and can be made more comprehensible only by interdisciplinary work.

Among the readings used in the seminar was a talk on the "Ontogeny of Ritualization in Man," which I had contributed to a symposium at the Royal Society of London in 1965.[2] The concept of ritualization has proved so essential a link between the ontogeny and the phylogeny of human playfulness that I have expanded it for inclusion in this text.

I learned much from our seminar; but in the end it seemed best, in this slim volume, to try to restate primarily my main themes and to suggest their variable applicability. As far as I myself was able to come closer to political vision proper, I have carried the matter somewhat further in the Jefferson Lectures, which I gave in 1973 for the National Endowment for the Humanities.[3] These lectures succeeded the Godkin Lectures in delivery and yet have preceded them in publication because of a special clause in the Jefferson lectureship. I hope that interested readers will be patient with a certain unavoidable overlapping in these publications.

My special acknowledgments must begin with the expression of my gratitude to Harvard University for the honor and pleasure of being invited back from retirement to give the Godkin Lectures. Dean Don K. Price of the Joseph F. Kennedy School of Government was a most attentive host. My former associate at Harvard, Pamela Daniels, organized the Godkin seminars with her special skill in inspiring collaboration in individuals from different fields.

My work on this book was much facilitated by a grant given by the Maurice Falk Foundation to the Department of Psychiatry at the Mt. Zion Hospital in San Francisco. My neighbor, Sherrill Brooks, typed—and retyped—the manuscript with care and understanding. My friends Kai T.

Erikson, Nathan Hale, Gerald Holton, Neil Smelser, and Robert Wallerstein have given the manuscript, or parts of it, critical readings. If I have not heeded all their warnings, the blame is mine.

Finally, as always, I thank Joan Erikson for her collaboration in my writings in many tangible and intangible ways. This book is dedicated to her because of her lifelong devotion to the grace that is play.

ERIK H. ERIKSON

Tiburon, California, 1975

I

Play and Vision

Introduction:
From Child's Play to Politics?

OF ALL THE FORMULATIONS of play, the briefest and the best is to be found in Plato's *Laws*. He sees the model of true playfulness in the need of all young creatures, animal and human, to leap. To truly leap, you must learn how to use the ground as a springboard, and how to land resiliently and safely. It means to test the leeway allowed by given limits; to outdo and yet not escape gravity. Thus, wherever playfulness prevails, there is always a surprising element, surpassing mere repetition or habituation, and at its best suggesting some virgin chance conquered, some divine leeway shared. Where this "happens," it is easily perceived and acknowledged.

But even play, in its many spontaneous and ritualized forms, has been drawn into human conflict. Plato, too, speaks of *young* creatures; and what seems to become of play as we grow older depends very much on our changing conceptions of the relationship of childhood to adulthood and, of course, of play to work. Adults through the ages have been inclined to judge play to be neither serious nor useful, and thus unrelated to the center of human tasks and motives, from which the adult, in fact, seeks "recreation" when he plays. Such a division makes life simpler and permits adults to avoid the often awesome suggestion that playfulness—and, thus, indeterminate chance—may occur in the vital center of adult concerns, as it does in the center of those of children. But even the vast literature on children's play reflects an intense ambivalence. Some of the play theories advanced seem to meet a passionate counter-Calvinist need to declare that all play at all ages must be altogether an end in itself, and a divine one, at that. On the other hand, developmental theories have marked the child's play as a prime necessity for growing and learning, while clinical theories have burdened it with the tasks of solving weighty inner problems indeed: we will come to that.

The designation "play," however, is also used for deceptions and pretenses, which deny rather than transcend reality; and here I would single out two rather divergent trends in our civilization, namely, a new and widespread tendency to play at being playful, and to simulate, sometimes with the help of alcohol or drugs, a repertory of roles (say, in sexual and communal "games"), often making demands beyond the emotional means of most. On the other hand, there is the grim determination of adults to "play roles"—that is, to impersonate to the point of no return their places in a cast forced upon them by what they consider inescapable reality.

Let me, in this introduction, concentrate on a trend in public consciousness that has seemed especially pronounced in recent national crises, namely, a general suspicion of playacting in high places indeed, and of the power of contrived scenarios not compatible with traditional national scripts. This imagery, so I noted as I was preparing for these lectures, was reflected with some regularity in the daily press. Having retired from Harvard, I could on occasion even manage to peruse the Sunday papers. And it did appear that themes somehow related to play in all its various meanings of grossly deceptive as well as imaginative make-believe characterized the mood of the commentators at that time, as if there were some pervasive sadness over the loss of playful leeway, some deep anger over the use of playacting for deception, and a universal, if vague, nostalgia for some kind of new "vision." Now, it is obvious that any quotations from the daily press of a given year soon appear dated; yet they may also illustrate some tenacious long-range trend. And one may well wonder whether ever before in history commentators of stature have been pre-occupied in equal measure with reality and irreality, with rationality and madness, with credibility, half-truth, and lying, and, above all, with scripts and scenarios. The American Dream, some insisted, was now a "nightmare"; credibility was said to be suffering not only from a gap but from an "abyss"; governmental deception, far from occasional, was felt to be spreading like "quicksand" under the feet of all.[1]

But let me quote a few diverse and yet representative examples of what I read at the time. To begin with the "legitimate" stage, a review by Walter Kerr of Archibald

MacLeish's *Scratch* was captioned, "But we have lost the faith." Kerr, focusing on a rocking horse in the center of the stage set, mused:

> Mr. MacLeish's rhythms, once our own, had—before our eyes and to the astonishment of our ears—become rocking horse rhythms, lulling sounds we had somewhere left behind, intonations gone to sleep along with certain of our certainties.[2]

To proceed to what we only metaphorically refer to as theaters, such as the "theater of war," some columnists made similarly despairing remarks which implied that a scenario had lost its meaning, a game its logic, and playfulness its spirit. It was the time of the Pentagon Papers. Hannah Arendt, in an incisive article,[3] emphasized not so much the governmental deceits perpetrated on the public as the self-deceit of the perpetrators. She suspected that in modern politics the deceivers *start* with *self*-deception, so that "the actors themselves no longer know or remember the truth behind their concealments and their lies," thus "losing contact with reality and, in fact, borrowing scenarios and audiences from the theater."[4] And, indeed, a direct quote from the Pentagon Papers shows that those self-deceiving problem-solvers endeavored to play up at one and the same time to relevant audiences on opposing sides of the foreign and the domestic scene: "the Communists (who must feel strong pressure), the South Vietnamese (whose morale must be buoyed), our allies (who must trust us as 'underwriters'), and the U.S. public (which must support the risk-taking with U.S. lives and prestige)."[5]

Arendt suggested two conclusions relevant to us: these deceits, in some significant historical way, go beyond "the background of past history, itself not exactly a story of immaculate virtue," and yet betray a fundamental trend in the human mind:

> The ability to lie, the deliberate denial of factual truth, and the capacity to change facts, the ability to act, are interconnected; they owe their existence to the same source, imagination. Hence, when we talk about lying, and especially about lying among acting men, let us remember that the lie did not creep into politics by some accident of human sinfulness; moral outrage, for this reason alone, is not likely to make it disappear.[6]

This, it seems to me, is where we come in: what, indeed, is this fundamental trend in the human mind, that capacity for imagining different scenarios which may serve as make-believe in the search for a fitting vision and yet can take over to the point where the cognitive as well as the emotional quality of action is changed?

In this connection, so-called game theories have come in for special criticism. As Tom Wicker put it, "Its perpetrators seem no longer to see [the war] as a war but as a gaming board; its bombs are merely signals to them and its deaths have nothing to do with life." [7]

George W. Ball, a man who was there when and where it happened, published a remarkable column, called "The Trap of Rationality," [8] in which he took issue with what was captioned as the "Think-Tank War," and what he referred to as the dialectic of the Pentagon Papers, that is, the application of game theory and model building to warfare. We do not question here the technical usefulness of scenarios in the hands of skilled and responsible professionals. At stake is, rather, the "natural" power of scenarios over those who so desperately want to believe that their technical properties make them more real than reality. Complaining that they "led to an obsession with the purely operational aspects of the Vietnamese struggle," Ball comes to this memorable conclusion:

What misled a group of able and dedicated men was that, in depersonalizing the war and treating it too much as an exercise in the deployment of resources, we ignored the one supreme advantage possessed by the other side: the non-material element of will, of purpose and patience, of cruel but relentless commitment to a single objective. . . . Yet that was the secret of North Vietnamese success—a rebuke of the spirit to the logic of number.[9]

I am quoting these commentators now primarily for their use of metaphors which then apparently were meaningful to their own and to the public's mood—and which are now useful for our theoretical intentions. The discomfort manifested in the remarks I have cited has certainly not been cured by the way in which, some time later, a week in Peking "changed history." It began in best McLuhanesque fashion, with a superbly staged television show witnessed on their home screens by millions all over the globe, but not shared by the visited population close by. And, as the Bamboo Curtain between two of the most populous nations on earth was so demonstratively lifted, our own John K. Fairbank concluded:

Since our images of distant realities change so much faster than the realities could possibly change themselves, we are left with simple logical alternatives: either we are stupid about China now, or we were stupid during those long years of cold war when our allies, Britain and France, were less so.[10]

This television show was only the most visible instance in a series of events which made it appear that to speak of a theater of history is by no means a mere metaphor any more.[11]

But to glance at the other end of the political spectrum and at those Americans who opposed the Vietnam war, there was, to be sure, a genuinely playful element in the marches and demonstrations, and we have every reason to believe that it was the spontaneity of nonviolent action which sometimes put the burden of lawless excess on the authorities and helped to alert the political imagination of many Americans. In the present context, however, we remember how a vociferous minority transformed another age-old "stage" of ritual conduct, namely, the courtroom, into a theater for the display of improvised comedy. There is, of course, a traditional scenario of mockery in castles, in the theater, and in circuses where clowns are employed for the purpose of mocking artfully (and safely) both the pretense of the robed bearers of power and the powerlessness of the governed. John Leonard, in reviewing a book called *The Tales of Hoffman* which dealt with the trial (presided over by erratic Judge Hoffman) of the "Chicago 8," a group accused of crossing a state line conspiring in their hearts to disrupt a political convention, comes to a tragic conclusion. The defendants, it will be remembered, tried to make of their political trial a farce, which Leonard compares to the living theater and other avant-garde dramatic presentations: everybody gets into the act. And he muses:

But at issue, in reality, was a law that seemed to say you can be crossing state lines in an invisible frame of mind. If everybody hadn't turned the trial into a guerrilla circus, we might have tested that law. It's still on the statute books, against which we pit joke-books.[12]

And, indeed, political role acting and playful protest have confronted each other in recent history in some rather contrived scenarios, some of which posed as revolutionary events. I am thinking here of the time, not so easily forgotten by those who were then in academic life, when a certain historical playfulness met head on with political facts. Take, for example, the revolutionary student at Columbia University whose picture made the papers in 1968, as he was "occupying President Grayson Kirk's office chair while puffing one of Kirk's 'liberated' cigars." Reinterviewed by *Time*, that former student, who is now intent on "creating a new poetry, a new cinema, a new voice," refers to that episode as "mock Theater." [13]

For him, all may be well that ends well. But a generation's memory cannot afford to pass over so easily events like the "occupations," which at the time masqueraded as a historical equivalent of the Bolsheviks' storming of the Winter Palace. If such events so soon thereafter appear to have been mock theater, they also resulted, in spite of some undeniable political impact, in a certain paralysis of youthful action, as if a cast of actors had awakened on a crowded stage without a guiding master script—and had dispersed. This young hero may have found his way to poetry proper. Others, no doubt, were dispirited enough to take their places in role assignments closer to an established "reality" in which they yet did not feel especially real.

Turning from protest to affirmation, in recent years many a traditional setting has been transformed by a playful improvisation which seems to renew a communal spirit long thought lost. Consider the traditional "concert" setting where a new kind of ecstatic "people," far from acting as a genteel and docile audience coming to life only by clapping at prescribed times, participated in the musical rhythms. Or think of the methods, imported from the East, of bringing some ignored resources of mental and physical being into play by meditation; or of the improvised versions of traditional ceremonies which are permitted in order to regenerate the ecumenical spirit in church life itself. There are also, within this cultivation of a more relevant, a more playful actuality, movements and terminologies which attempt to expose the unconscious "games people play"—a use of both the terms "game" and "play" which more or less mockingly betrays the "deals" in familial politics. Yet, some of our most extreme advocates of gamesmanship (in sexuality and in religion, in therapy and in business) cannot hide for long the strenuousness in some of their simulated joy and the exhaustion in such hard-won relaxation, not to speak of the aftereffects of the chemical means which are so often needed for a subjective sense of existence as a playground.

In this wide range of phenomena, what seems to be at stake is the mutual legitimation of playful imagination and of factual reality, and thus the credibility of reality itself and of play itself. All this perplexing intelligence—which certainly calls for a concerted effort at interpretation by a variety of disciplines—seemed to sanction my taking another look at the ontogeny of play and its offspring, the ritualization of everyday life throughout the life cycle.

One reservation: A moment ago, I called the Great Peking Broadcast "McLuhanesque"; and I must admit that one could view the credibility gap illustrated here only as a side issue in an otherwise grandiose change in human nature, consequent to the modern "information environment" which "alters our concepts and our entire perceptual life." Or, as I heard McLuhan say more recently, "Instant electric information constitutes a new acoustic or resonant space whose center is everywhere and whose margin is nowhere." This resonant space, he believes, is a discontinuum which "hijacks private self-identity, the supreme artifact of Western man." [14] In contrast, however, to thinkers who give their full attention to the changing world of technocratic facts and to the seemingly infinite leeway in man's transformation, psychologists like myself are ever and again impressed with those ontogenetic and emotional givens in man's life cycle and in the structure of his institutions which carry over into the technocratic age and may, in fact, point to an all the more desperate need for a "real" identity in the very world of artifacts. Such basic needs, we must insist, change only at an infinitesimally slow rate, and one suspects that a sense of reality—and with it a sense of playful mastery —depends on the relative relation of that which must repeat itself from generation to generation to what is truly new from era to era. In this sense, I intend to take another look at the evolutionary and ontogenetic beginnings of human play. What relation may there be (beyond mere metaphor) between the playing child and the playacting adult; between make-believe and belief; between the legitimate theater and what we call the theaters of politics and war; between playful vision and serious theory: between the child's toys, then, and aged reason? Here I must touch on a number of fields while I can offer only one set of observations originating in what the play of children and the dreams of patients have taught me about the basic human need for a shared vision of reality.

But before I leave the political scene for an extended excursion into our ontogenetic beginnings, let me conclude my introduction by commenting on an astounding commentator. It was the late Walter Lippmann who fifty

years ago formulated (well, almost) the theme to which
I hope to gain access. In his classic book *Public Opinion*,
and in a chapter called "The World Outside and the Pictures in Our Heads," he examined "how opinions are crys-
tallized into what is called Public Opinion, how a National
Will, a Group Mind, a Social Purpose, or whatever you
choose to call it is formed," [15] and he took psychoanalysis
to task in a way that must interest us here and now. "The
psychoanalyst," he claimed, "almost always assumes that
the environment is knowable, and if not knowable, then
at least bearable, to any unclouded intelligence." [16]

The psychoanalyst examines the adjustment to an X, called by him
the environment; the social analyst examines the X, called by him
the pseudo-environment.[17]

Since then, many articles and books have been written
which have focused on the power of political images and
on "scratches on the mind," on political moods as well as
perceptions and misconceptions, on politics and pseudo-
politics. My "psycho-historical" friends have begun to develop psychoanalytic insights clarifying not only what
imagination contributes to the structure of that vague
phenomenon of a "public mind," but also how the public
sphere reaches into the ontogenetic beginnings and the emotional life of the individual. It is the more remarkable that
Walter Lippmann fifty years ago had already stated the
problem succinctly:

The real environment is altogether too big, too complex, and too
fleeting for direct acquaintance. And although we have to act in
that environment, we have to reconstruct it on a simpler model before we can manage with it. The analyst of public opinion must begin, then, by recognizing the triangular relationship between the
scene of action, the human picture of that scene, and the human response to that picture working itself out upon the scene of action.[18]

And he, the political commentator, comes to a conclusion which we might say is really beyond his competency, were it not that it challenges us to make a leap worth trying.

The range of fiction extends all the way from complete hallucinations to the scientists' perfectly self-conscious use of a schematic model. . . . The very fact that men theorize at all is proof that their pseudo-environments, their interior representations of the world, are a determining element in thought, feeling and action.[19]

While this last quotation suggests a wide range for our deliberations, the comments quoted earlier all seem to confirm that political life can be experienced by some who observe it most closely and who, we would expect, feel most familiar in it, as a scene of activity which does not live up to some preconceived vision—not to speak of a national dream—and yet also falls ruefully short of "real" reality. Now, I know as well as the next man that at their most pragmatic many observers would simply admit, if not boast, that, yes, this is what politics is all about.[20] But why, then, should our seasoned commentators lament this fact, and why should they circumscribe it in terms of play, games, and ritual, or of dream and nightmare? Since I come from a field which specializes in the observation of play and dreams, and this in clinical contact with matters of utmost consequence for human fate, I will attempt in this book to clarify the relation of play to reality in different stages of life and in various compartments of human existence—including, eventually, the politics of everyday life and at least approaching "real" politics.

The Toy Stage

WE WILL FIRST WATCH one child's quiet arrangement of
toys on a small table. In a modern school, cooperative in
such matters, we invited one child at a time to leave his
play group and come to a room where a table and a set
of blocks awaited him. The person who fetched him sat
down on the floor with him and asked him to "build something" and to "tell a story" about it. Another observer sat
in a corner recording what happened.

This method of "play construction," it should be noted,
is only one variation of a number of much more ambitious
investigative techniques in which many more toys of a
strictly selected variety are used for clinical investigation.
In England, Margaret Lowenfeld, several decades ago,
even established a method called "The World Test" by
which she undertook to study "the structure of the mind

in childhood." Kamp and Kessler say of this last method that

> . . . most children tend to handle these larger collections of small toys in a work-like manner rather than playfully. And although few would agree that play characteristics are totally absent from these test situations, the children seem to be intensively preoccupied with the end product, i.e., "making something." [21]

In other words, confronted with an all too ready-made toy "world" (houses, trees, and fences, in addition to people, vehicles, and animals), the children seem to be most eager to show that they know how to arrange them in a functional way. More like a test, then, their performance reflects primarily their mental capacity (or incapacity) to organize a classified universe. In comparison, the inventory presented here, in addition to a cast of small dolls, offers a certain number of simple blocks in the hope that our instructions will induce the child to structure the available space with original configurations and then to confabulate freely.

In my own experience, then, this is not an "experiment," but a proven clinical method applied to developmental observation. Small patients, it is well known, in their fright and confusion turn to available playthings with a desperate neediness, often confessing and expressing on the toy stage much more than they could possibly say or probably know "in that many words." Just because such observation is a clinical tool, however, it is important to record that *all* children but the most inhibited ones go at the opportunity of arranging toys on a small stage with a specific confabulatory eagerness, some more somberly and systematically, others with a "flash" of a sudden "idea." Depending on their age, some may bid for time by first asking some questions or handling some toys (in which case their initial selections can be quite suggestive), but soon they become absorbed in a task governed by some imperative theme and by a certain sense of style until the construction is suddenly declared finished, often with an expression of posture and face which seems to say that *this* is *it*—and it is good. If I repeat here an impressive example already presented previously,[22] I do so in order to illustrate the great number of significant themes which can become apparent in the repeated study of one play event.

The child is a five-year-old black boy, Robert, who, we have been warned, is apt to enter any room with the energetic question, "Where is the action?" And, indeed, he loses no time over questions and explorations, and immediately erects a high, symmetrical, and well-balanced block structure in the middle of the table.

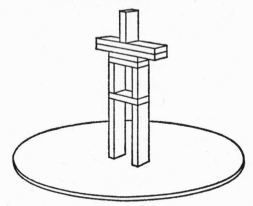

Appearing pleased, he now scans the other toys and, with quick, categorical moves, first distributes the toy *vehicles* on the floors and ledges of the block structure. Next, he groups all the *animals* together in a *scene beside the tower*, the snake seeming to be the center of their joined attention.

Now he pauses more pensively and then chooses as his *first human figure* the *black boy*, whom he lays on the very top of the building. The other human dolls follow: the youngest dolls are laid into the vehicles as if into beds, and some authoritative men figures (doctor, policeman, old man) are put on top of them, like the incubi of old, the demons in a nightmare—but facing up. The other human dolls are then stood up in a half circle around the animal scene, their *arms lifted*, as if in some excitement.

The boy's "story" is one of the briefest: "Cars come to the house. The lion bites the snake, who wiggles his tail. The monkey and the kitten try to kill the snake. People come to watch. Little one [black boy] on the roof is where smoke comes out."

In attempting to classify such a construction, one can emphasize countable *common elements* displayed by a certain number of children in a given cultural setting, or of the same age or sex. Or one could concentrate on one or another symbol such as the snake, which typically represents a creature intent on harm, and here, too, arouses violent reactions, uniting other animals in the wish to do away with it: it would then depend on our theoretical inclination and credulity to decide whether the snake represents just any sneaky kind of danger, Evil Incarnate, a phallic symbol—or maybe all of these together. One could rate the use of blocks and the style of distribution of other toys. Here I would judge the boy's scene to be markedly boyish and definitely advanced for his age. But, as I said, for any "clinical" method, even if applied to developmental data, a prime tool for interpretation is the establishment of one or another *unique element* in the construction. And this, it so happens, is the only scene in hundreds in which the dolls stand with arms stretched out. Such a unique element usually provides clues, and, indeed, we are now struck with the fact that the block structure *itself* somehow resembles (if in the rigid, simplistic manner of blocks) a standing body with arms stretched out sidewise. There are, of course, similar towers in other constructions, but this one has the longest armlike extrusions. And if this "is" a body, then the black boy doll is where the head is.

Uniqueness owes its significance to thematic similarities in different compartments of a life history. When we showed a series of such constructions to the teachers in this boy's school, one of them remarked that this boy can compete with much older ones in physical strength and grace. And she noted that he often does a peculiar thing: with a detached smile, he dances a two-step around the classroom with his arms stretched out sideways. As the teacher mimicked his posture with delight (theirs is an "open" classroom), all the little toys with outstretched arms, and even the ponderous block configuration, seemed to come to life. Once, the teacher continued, she had congratulated the boy on his athletic ability and on the gracefulness of his dancing motions; but he had responded with a despairing gesture and had said, "Yes, but my brain is no good." Whereupon she had assured him that this was exactly what the school was for: to help body and brain to help each other.

This kind of data can arouse in clinical workers a strong and immediate impression which they can then proceed to fortify as other impressions "fall in place." If we assume, then, the building to be a body, and the boy doll to be where the head is, then the whole construction may well echo the teacher's formula for the solution of what worried the boy at the time, namely, how to keep body and brain together and to make them work in concert. This we came to accept as the central theme which holds all the smaller ones together: the boy's hope to manage all the critical issues in his life with the formula of a unified body and mind. I am reminded here of something Piaget said: "In order for a child to understand something, he must construct it himself, he must re-invent it." [23]

Thus, there is more to a play construction than a grandiose restoration of narcissistic self-esteem. The details, whether unique or typical, pointedly indicate some of the experiential dimensions which must be "held together" by the adaptive formula. In psychoanalytic terms, we see the ego at work; and it must be our endeavor to recognize in a given playful construction the basic way in which the experiences of a stage of life and of a state of conflict are translated into and reconciled in a specific space-time arrangement. Let us, then, play with the themes suggested.

The over-all configuration of our construction expresses the truly basic developmental fact of childhood, namely, that the human being in growing up must learn to master to the point of free and unrestrained motion the evolutionary gift of an erect bipedal posture, and with it a basic space-time orientation. With his stereoscopic vision and his alert imagination, the human being learns to orient himself in his kind of space and time: "looking forward" to what is in front and what is ahead and turning backward on what is behind and in back. Combining values with directions, he learns to look up to what is above, higher, and highest, and down to what is below, lower, and lowest. But such upright orientation also creates a stark right and left; and, eventually, strong connotations of social and

sexual differentiation become attached to all these directions.

In our example, we find related to the image of the erect
posture those symbols and themes we have learned to consider typical for the *locomotor* and *genital* stage of psychosexual development, with its intense sexual curiosity—and
curious apprehensions. The configuration of the authoritative incubi on top of the infants is, in fact, a totally unique
configuration among the bedroom scenes of the play constructions known to me: but whatever inner apprehension
it may reflect, it is obviously an archetypal theme of ancient standing. The phallic theme, in turn, becomes truly
prominent if we look at the block structure, as it were, in
profile. We then see the fire truck's ladder—an erectable
item par excellence—protrude horizontally, thus emphasizing the general theme of unrestrained bodily extension,
arms and all. The opposite theme of lowness we see not
only in the infant-succubi who are "below," but also in
the "lowest" creature of them all, the earthbound snake
which is looked down on by the excited human beings and
is cornered and attacked by all the other animals (led by
the highest of these, the kingly lion). But if these configurations represent the instinctual dangers and fantasies
of the phallic stage, we see a serious remnant of its basic
conflict in the fact that the black boy on the very *top* of
the construction lies supine. Robert has proven that he
knows how to stand these toys up even with arms extended:
is the highest and most exposed of them in the greatest
danger of falling down?

I have ascribed to this stage of life the *psychosocial* op-
posites of *initiative* and *guilt*. It is clear that both the dancing posture and the teacher's formula open up initiatives

both in work and in play, and for both mind and body. On the other hand, even as the fate of the snake may represent punishment for phallic guilt, the incubi, in addition to some sexual theme, suggest the oppressive threat of authority—policeman, doctor, "old man." (There could, in fact, hardly be a better configuration for the "super" ego heavily lording it over the as yet immature ego.) The rudimentary strength emerging from the conflicts of this stage is *purposefulness*, and we are mindful of Robert's favorite inquiry, "Where is the action?"

If, finally, we have learned to call this stage the Oedipus stage because of the prevalence of the supreme hybris of fantasies of replacing the father in all his top positions and of having exclusive possession of the mother, we may remember here that the theme of the erect human posture pervades the whole Oedipus myth as well: the very name means "swollen foot," for the explicit reason that his feet had been pierced before his abandonment in order to prevent in his grown-up life the sinful initiatives predicted by the oracle.

To compare any unique construction with others equally unique would be a time-consuming thing, and so I must ask readers to accept this one performance as an example of a five-year-old's eagerness and capacity to use a toy inventory on a given table for a relevant and yet probably only vaguely conscious "statement" which dramatizes the solution of a deep uncertainty—an uncertainty which, we may now add, is not restricted to this one boy and his individual fantasy life: for many black youngsters share the dilemma of a relative imbalance of their physical vigor, their power of expression, and a certain inhibition in school learning. Singular in this case is the fact that the boy found words for it and entrusted them to the teacher, that the teacher found a significant answer, and that the boy could express it in his construction.

But if the teacher's remark amounted to such a meaningful communication, they did so not only as a personal expression but also as a message signifying some changes in over-all world view—changes which in the teacher's and the boy's lifetime had been brought about by the civil rights movement on the one hand, and by modern education on the other. I will later discuss what I will call the everyday ritualization of the educative process: only an open classroom could permit and encourage indulgence in a dance step—and promise its siynchronization with the use of mental faculties.

The play construction, then, can be seen to be inventively negotiating between the small builder's inner universe and his society's changing world view. I have used it, therefore, as an introduction to some formulations concerning the individual ego's space-time, which, as I will try to make plausible, lives in constant interplay with the space-time of established or evolving world views.

In clinical work, we have learned to take it for granted that in play as well as in dreams pervasive uncertainties and wished-for solutions should find a more or less transparent representation. But that a child not pathologically disturbed could and would use a toy microsphere and a few minutes with a receptive observer to dramatize a central conflict may be harder to believe. If I ever doubted it, I learned better when recently I had an opportunity to review the lives of some of the Berkeley children who had done such play constructions for me thirty years ago.[24] This was possible only because the Institute of Human Development at the University of California has carried out one of the most significant "longitudinal" studies in history, collecting a wealth of data not only throughout the first two decades of life, but also following them up on the occasion of these children's thirtieth and fortieth birthdays. Fate and history, it can be imagined, have offered these people much unpredictable support and hindrance, which each absorbed in his own individual way: but these personal ways had retained, it now became clear, a remarkable thematic closeness to the content and the form of the play constructions which in a few minutes they had put on a table for me when they were twelve years old.

But let me choose an example from a context familiar to some readers. Take the black boy mentioned in *Childhood and Society* who confessed that sometimes before falling asleep, he liked to listen to "The Lone Ranger," but that he had found himself suddenly turning the program off because he realized that, most inappropriately, he had begun to imagine the Lone Ranger to be himself—and black. At that time, he reported this smilingly; he seemed to have the problem well in hand. He, too, produced some play constructions for me in his early teens. His block structures on two occasions were especially original and well-built configurations—all representing cages which contained wild animals watched over by uniformed figures and dogs: "A zoo," was all he could say by way of a story. The constricted theme and the whole configuration then seemed sadly fitting for his eminently "contained" exterior. Yet the quality of his play reflected much talent.

Recently, and more than thirty years later, I had occasion to visit this man in the city to which he had moved. He had made a special name for himself because of his ability under the most trying circumstances to befriend and to guide groups of black teen-agers about to get involved in destructive (and self-destructive) activity. I found him to be an impressively handsome and strong man who remembered having met me but had (as is most often the case) only the vaguest memory of having done play constructions for me. Nor did he ask me what he had constructed. But when I now inquired what he thought had given him the strength to guide youngsters in a riotous mood, he said something like this: "These boys can see that I am strong and they feel that I have it in me to be violent myself. But they also know that I have my anger well in hand and that they could never provoke me to act against my values. So they listen to me." This is as good a statement on nonviolence as I have heard; but it also seemed quite consonant with the repetitive theme of the play constructions he had done when he was in his early teens, the theme of wildness contained and yet also transcended by discipline and self-expression.

Historical developments and a new political vision had permitted this man to go beyond the early solution of a smiling compliance: he had become aware of his anger and yet also learned to employ it in social action. As so often, his life, when compared with early observations, was an instance of a promise kept beyond prediction, and his play constructions had a recognizable place in that life history.

Seeing Is Hoping

I DO NOT KNOW how convincing two short examples of this kind can be to those who are not familiar with and already accepting of the psychoanalytic proposition that every human expression means more than it seems to say—and much more than it is consciously intended to say—and that such meaning can be shown to have central significance. And even if it is granted that something as complex as I have suggested may be "at work" in those toy scenes, one may wonder whether such strenuous meaning does not contradict the very idea of play as a God-given gift. A theologian once called me a spoilsport because I have presumed, too, to detect conflict and purpose even in children's play. And, as I have admitted, clinical and other theories have burdened child's play with formidable tasks. According to the "traumatic" theory, it serves the compulsion to repeat symbolically experiences not sufficiently managed in the past, and to turn what was passively suffered into a theme of active mastery. The "cathartic" theory sees in play primarily a function in the present, namely, the release of some pent-up emotion or the release of surplus energy that cannot be put into the service of what is serious and useful. Then again, there are "functional" theories which see in play an exercise of new faculties, and thus a preparation for the future. Now, while none of these theories tells the whole story, I would not be ready to discard any of them, because they all point to factors omnipresent in all human thought and action. But if we acknowledge in certain play events the "working through" of some traumatic experience, we also note that the very factor of playfulness transforms them into acts of renewal. If some such events seem to be governed by a need to communicate, or even to confess something, the element of playfulness adds the joy of self-expression. And if play so obviously helps the exercise of growing faculties, it does so with inventiveness and abandon. In fact, where any of these gifts is severely handicapped, as is, of course, all too common in our small patients, the child is apt to suffer from what I have termed "play disruption." Unimpaired playfulness, however, not only endows events categorized as play; it is so much a part of being active and alive that it soon tends to elude any definition except, perhaps, one that can include this elusive quality—as does Plato's "leap."

About this there will be much more to say later. Right now, let me return once more to our play constructions and to one of their prime characteristics. For out of the vast array of phenomena which are called play, or look like play, or feel like play, our illustrations exemplify a specific human capacity, grounded in man's evolution and developed in the toy world of childhood imagination, namely, to use objects endowed with special and symbolic meanings for the representation of an imagined scene in a circumscribed sphere. In our instance, such scenes are induced by adult request and, therefore, can not be considered to be altogether spontaneous. In fact, we could go further (and will do so later) and call what took place here a ritualized procedure. And yet, one will grant these constructions that element of true playfulness which alone can give them their quality of surprise both in form and in content. More, the probable meaning we have ascribed to the toy scenes represents the dare of a new chance: what if one could, indeed, learn to let mind and body truly interplay; or to create a new social gift out of years of overly disciplined self-restriction!

In any toy procedure, then, we emphasize a *spatial aspect* which the great theorist of play, Huizinga, encompasses in a sweeping summary: "All play moves and has its being within a playground marked off beforehand, either materially or ideally, deliberately or as a matter of course." [25] He names an array of phenomena that share this characteristic: "The arena, the card-table, the magic circle, the temple, the stage, the screen, the tennis court, the court of justice, etc., are all in form and function, playgrounds . . . isolated, hedged round, hallowed, within which special rules obtain." All these he calls "temporary worlds within the ordinary world, dedicated to the performance of an act apart." [26]

We will make our own selection of playgrounds as we proceed. Right now, we want only to point to a special relation between the toy stage and the child's time-space experience. As I put it in *Childhood and Society*, such "dramatic" play in childhood provides the *infantile form of the human propensity to create model situations in which aspects of the past are re-lived, the present re-presented and renewed, and the future anticipated.* Let me begin to expand on this over-all theme while we still have our play construction before us.

There is a *central conflict*, characteristic of the *developmental crisis* being lived through by the child. In Robert's construction, the tall structure, as we claimed, represents a dancing gesture of locomotor self-assertion which might help overcome the conflicts and traumata alluded to in the side scenes. In the center is the image of a boy-in-the-making, who will learn new ways of integrating bodily grace and vigor with the capacity to comprehend and to learn. But, as we noted, this boy's uneasiness over the reconciliation of bodily expression and mental discipline extends to much of his cultural and historical setting. This *puer novus*, in fact, contains a nascent image of a *homo novus*, a liberated adult. If so, the words of the teacher are somehow present as a prophecy of a new communal sponsorship. The total event, then, is an experimentation in the microsphere with a new identity element embedded in a new sense of community. Such a basic spatial theme, however, contains some temporal coordinates relating past traumata and solutions to fearful as well as hopeful aspects of the future. Here we could only surmise that the boy's original complaint to the teacher contained some such fears as: What if he is doomed by some "fixating" past, and cannot make the body and the mind work together? And what if he now tries to be a new boy, but circumstances beyond his control will refuse to sponsor him? Will he be and remain nobody, and amount to nothing? And yet, the demonstrative dancing with outstretched arms and an angelic smile also expresses a sense of having been loved sometime by somebody as one with new and special gifts: without some such past experience, there is little future. Thus, the recapitulation of a possible doom is turned into a promised renewal through playful mastery in the present: maybe one will grow up to be whole, and there is a chance of growing up loving and lovable. Such an implicit formula, I think, causes the often unforgettable smile on the face of many children (I would call it inwardly triumphant) when they declare their construction to be "all done."

I know that I am using rather mythical words here—too mythical for a child's vocabulary, but not, I would think, for his experiential feelings. For in infantile play we see the ontogeny of a human propensity which throughout life will be shared in a widening arena of interplay, namely, to construct visual models which will be "recognized" by peers and teachers who thus will help the playing child to do what he cannot do alone for long, namely, come to terms with a sense of dread and regain belief in a utopian promise; to feel reassured of the chance of subduing destructive forces within and fighting off inimical ones without and thus to continue to feel like a new being capable of utilizing new competencies in a widening present. These big words for wordless play are used here so that later we may proceed to recognize such themes in the shared visions of adulthood. It would, at any rate, be underestimating the infantile antecedents of the experience of existential dread or confidence were we to exclude these aspects of our consciousness from a child's total, if as yet dim, awareness. Certainly, the universal character of fairy tales attests to such readiness.

If childhood play and the other spheres of playfulness as yet to be reviewed depend on a strong visual element, they are dominated also by an almost visionary fascination with the temporal fate of figures meaningfully arranged in a circumscribed "world." This combines the two meanings of vision, namely, the capacity to see what is before us, here and now, and the power to foresee what, if one can only believe it, might yet prove to be true in the future. To find the origin of these two aspects of human vision, we must go even further back in ontogeny and immerse ourselves in the earliest and least distinct beginnings.

In the Chicago symposium, René Spitz reported on his and his Denver colleagues' latest observations and speculations concerning the role of vision in the establishment of a rudimentary sense of reality in the infant.[27] It is the gift of vision, they point out, which first serves to integrate the messages received from the other senses: taste, audition, smell, and touch. "Vision introduces into the infant's world, in which so far contact perception predominated, the new and fateful distance perception. Because of distance perception the child begins to understand continuity in time and coherence in space." [28] By the third month, so Spitz claims, the infant's visual discrimination has matured sufficiently to permit him to remember a total gestalt; and it stands to reason that the visual percepts now to be integrated and retained have been associated with the vital pleasures of oral and sensory satisfactions: those of being fed and held, touched, cleaned, and "tucked in." Through all of these administrations, the motherly person lets her face "shine upon" the newborn's searching eyes; she thus lets herself be verified as the first comprehensible image. And, indeed, once infants can nurse with open eyes, they are apt to stare at the mother's face even as they suck on her breast. Thus vision becomes the leading perceptual as well as emotional modality for the organization of a sensory and sensual space as marked by the infant's interplay with the *primal person*. To believe this, we need only to enumerate what vision manages to confirm: simultaneity in time as well as continuity in space, permanence of objects as well as coherence of the perceived field, the foreground figure and the fusion of the background, the motion of some items against the stationary position of others—and all this held together by the desired presence of the providing person. This, I believe, is the model of what later is felt to be the "really real" enveloping the mere factual. Soon, of course, audition will prove essential and useful because it permits one to hear what is not in the visual field, and thus reinforces the hope that the voice heard will come "around the corner" and be confirmed as the familiar face. This double perception of the primary parent as both seen and heard is further verified as that person ever again vocally "recognizes" the infant by some appellation which becomes a name even as the naming person is pleased to be recognized as the recognizer. As Joan Erikson puts it: "We begin life with this relatedness to eyes. . . . It is with eyes that concern and love are communicated, and distance and anger, as well. Growing maturity does not alter this eye-centeredness, for all through life our social intercourse with others is eye-focussed: the eye that blesses and curses." [29]

In this joint domain of cognitive and affective growth, then, the power of vision in the two meanings mentioned emerges: that of comprehending what can be verified as factual with the maturing senses, but also that of foreseeing as attainable what is recognized as reliable enough to be repeated—ever again.

But what does all this have to do with play? In his Heinz Werner Lectures, Bruner claims that ". . . the infant sensory apparatus yields information far beyond the capacity of the motor apparatus to use it." [30] The result is "a prolonged period of scanning the environment without early motor commitment, so that the structure of space can be elaborated autonomously of action." [31] And in support of Spitz's contention of the primary importance of vision, let me describe Bruner's ingenious elaboration of an experiment: an infant of six weeks is linked up with a sucking mechanism, which, in turn, is connected with a projector so that the infant by sucking with varying intensities and speeds can cause a picture on a screen to become either blurred or clarified. Bruner concludes, ". . . from the start of human infancy, a good visual stimulus, concentrically organized and sharply contoured, will have the effect of inhibiting sucking altogether, suggesting that the epistemic needs of the newborn organism are not completely swamped by the need for food and comfort." [32]

One might postulate, then, that the infant's scanning search with his senses and above all, his eyes, and that his renewed recognition of what is continuously lost and found again, is the first significant *interplay* (later to be re-tested in such games as, say, peekaboo). It is crowned by the smile reliably aroused at about twelve weeks of age by the "sign gestalt" of the mother's face and is, of course, itself a potent evocatory stimulus in that it enhances the parental person's wish for a recognition (in every sense of the word) which only the newborn can convey. For the smiling infant (for sound reasons of survival) has the potential power to make the adult feel central and new.

And then there is always Piaget. At the very beginning of his *Construction of Reality in the Child*, he says, "A world composed of permanent objects constitutes . . . a spatial universe obeying the principle of causality . . . without continuous annihilations or resurrections. Hence it is a universe both stable and external, relatively distinct from the internal world and one in which the subject places himself as one particular term among all the other terms." [33] Note that in the middle of Piaget's discourse, governed as it is by *raison*, we suddenly find the existential words "annihilations" and "resurrections"—and we may well make the most of them. For I believe that what we have described here is and remains basic for man's spiritual needs—or, to put it more generally, it is basic not only for a sense of reality endowing with meaning what we are learning to see and "grasp," but also for that visionary propensity by which man in all subsequent stages restores a measure of feeling reasonably at home in a predictable world, and that is: to be central in his sphere of living rather than peripheral and ignored; active and effective rather than inactivated and helpless; selectively aware rather than overwhelmed by or deprived of sensations; and, above all, chosen and confirmed rather than bypassed and abandoned. The rudiments of all this are implied in the indistinct beginning of that consciousness which, in whatever language, learns to speak as "I" and in all religions seeks for a vision of sanctioned centrality. If, then, the face-to-face phenomena which René Spitz and Joan Erikson refer to are reminiscent of religious images (such as the inclined face of the Madonna and the aura of her oneness with the Child), they may well be the ontogenetic basis of faith—that belief in a centrality sanctioned by a divine "I"—which remains both elemental and fateful in man's search for charismatic leaders.

Psychosocially speaking, I have postulated that the rudiments of hope—the first psychosocial strength essential for ego development—arise out of a fundamental struggle between basic trust and basic mistrust in infancy, and that this first conflict, like all subsequent ones, must be re-solved throughout life. How, then, about Piaget's "annihilations"? How about the basic mistrust of things perceived as alien, the dread of the maternal face turned away, the fear of and the rage over an image of the primal Other that becomes elusive or distorted—and thus the threatening loss of a reassuring reality? Spitz early in his work postulated a specific "eighth month anxiety" in which the infant reacts to strangers with "apprenhensive frowns" or a "tearful outburst." We laugh; we say, "Silly baby"; we reassure. Yet that silly fear of the unfamiliar is only the first experience of alienation, a mixture of anxiety and rage which also persists into all later phases of life and can pervade a widening rage of relations: the anxiety, just when and because one grows up to be a person, of being abandoned by what has become familiar and of being left a victim to crushing forces; the terror of the evil eye and the dread of being alone in a universe without a supreme counterplayer, without charity.

We clinicians learn to know something of those "annihilating" beginnings when we are confronted with child patients in whom some experiential nutriment is defective because of some weakness in the early interplay described here. And we are confronted with it by young patients threatened by psychosis who demand from us a daily, hourly reassurance that they would not be devastated if they dared to love and be loved, nor that they would be destroyed by or, indeed, would destroy the loved one. We thus learn to grasp the fragility of that "I" with which we learn to begin so many utterances as we speak from a central "point of view" (a *Gesichtspunkt*, as the Germans call it) attesting to views more inclusive than the sum of the facts we can be sure of, and appealing for a communal actuality which must help coordinate our orientation.

Play's End

WE ARE NOW REACHING a critical moment not atypical for a psychoanalytic presentation. My attempt to outline the ontogenetic beginnings of the visual and the visionary aspects of playful imagination is hardly "off the ground" of the first phase of life, and I am beginning to approach the later stages with broad and hurried strokes. A possible emotional reason for our fixation on beginnings was well expressed recently in "Peanuts." Lucy, the doctor, was "in" and her advice was available for a pre-inflationary five cents. Little Linus introduced the therapeutic encounter with the claim that he felt he was now on the way to solving some of his childhood problems. Lucy approved forcefully: "That's good, Linus, because then you'll be ready for teen-age problems, young adult problems, marriage problems, middle-age problems, declining years and old age problems." There was a gasp and a silence. Then Linus, with his enigmatic expression of one caught between the wish to look backward and the necessity to look ahead, said, "Let's get back to my childhood problems."

There is, of course, some pervasive rationale for dwelling on ontogeny, for its early phases take up a goodly proportion of human life for reasons intrinsic to the nature of human evolution; and yet, that fatefulness throughout history has been ignored, repressed, and mythologized for the same reasons. As we wish to study, then, the ontogenetic origins of man's visions of himself, we must become aware of the possibility that over-all images of childhood, and age-old repressions concerning it, are and have always been important aspects of changing world views. The mere search for beginnings always harbors some vision of an innocence lost or a hidden curse to be dealt with—and both with some sense of inescapable predestination.

Freud, who never worked with children clinically, but deeply treasured their company in daily life, noted with bitter sadness what the process of growing up makes of what he called *"die strahlende Intelligenz des Kindes"*: the radiant intelligence of the child. And those of us who have observed children's play, including that of child patients in acute emotional conflict, have never been able to hide some rather elemental joy in seeing children look and speak, play and act with an originality and wholeness recovered only in creative moments in later life. I should admit, then, that work with children can reinforce a kind of creative creed that there is something in the nature of childhood play that is therapeutic in the deepest sense.

And yet, it was Freud who taught us the *clinical awareness* which confirms the fixative and regressive power in-

herent in the fact of man's prolonged childhood, including
the very condition of that deep habituation with make-
believe which can be so creatively playful and yet, as we
must also show, so destructively deceptive. For *developmental awareness* must show us how mankind (*homo ludens*
as well as *homo sapiens* and *homo erectus*) has played emotional games with the very fact of playfulness in assuming
that childhood is all play and make-believe (and therefore
the cradle of all poetry as well as all irresponsibility) while
adults are all serious and factual, except where they make an
(often strenuous) decision to be all play.

Reliable research, it would seem, is the best way to get at
the true nature of childhood. And yet, scientific search, too,
and especially where it concerns human existence, is itself
guided by preconceived visions. Only systematic awareness,
therefore, can help us clarify our adult attitudes toward the
child before—and within—us.

Evolutionary awareness might suggest that the very delight with what is young and playful may be built into us
as part of an instinctive response, necessary to the survival
of the species and counteracting the extreme hazards of
human infancy. But then, again, *historical awareness* impresses on us the fact that this potential delight and faith in
childhood has by no means always protected children
against physical abuse or against economic exploitation, or
against (more or less intentional) mental torture—and mur-
der. A new trend in the study of childhood speaks, in fact,
of the history of childhood as "a nightmare from which we
have only recently begun to awaken." [34]

The end of play, then, becomes an essential part of a
study of human play, as may be seen from the many con-
trary uses of the word "play" itself. We emphasize fair

play, for we know our propensity for foul play. Where
we can playfully pretend and sovereignly act "as if," we
can come to "play a role" and be taken in by it ourselves.
The very word *ludere* suggests that man's playfulness leads
him into il-lusions and his fantasy into de-lusion. And we
can collude with some to delude others. By the same token,
if every innocent play contains a "plot," so does a plotter's
scheme; and if a plan or blueprint has a design, so do
schemers have designs on others. We must, then, come to
grips with the ontogenetic sources of the aggressive and deceptive aspects of the human use of the natural propensity
for familial and communal interplay for, surely, it forms
one basis for what later becomes systematic and destructive
in politics in its most fashionable and its seemingly legitimate usage. In order to begin to clarify all this, it is first
of all essential to discuss the aggressive aspects of play—as
well as the playful aspects of aggression.

A fundamental and almost innocent "aggressivity" in-
forms every act of being alive—and thus also of being playful. It simply belongs to a growing organism's very existence
in space and time—and, indeed, *aggredere* means first and
foremost to *go at* things and people in a way that may
invite playful mutuality but may also interfere with their
leeway without being antagonistic in either intention or
affect. I call it "almost innocent," however, because in man
acts of reciprocal interference soon lead to experiences of
frustration and rage, shame and guilt. For it is a basic fact
of human existence that, while the individual needs leeway
in order to grow and to develop, he must from the start
learn to limit his ad-gression by absorbing into his behavior
and by taking into his conscience the mores of the cultural
setting, which, lacking the animal's instinctive embedded-

ness in a segment of nature, must provide boundaries and rules of interplay as well as a total world view promising some leeway for all as well as some sanctioned ways of usurpation for some.

The point, or one point, in going back to the ontogenetic beginnings of play, then, is to recognize beyond the myths of the past the fragility as well as the power of playfulness in the human condition, beginning with the patterns of mutual fittedness and of eager interplay between the newborn and the maternal environment. That early experience, as we saw, established the foundamental experience of a *reciprocity of function*, and of playfulness confirmed by *mutality*—an interplay which counteracts in childhood as it alleviates in later life the human readiness for bewildered reaction and rage.

It is true, of course, that the enchanting play of animals seems to exist within an order in which it remains clear (at any rate within the same species) under what conditions there is leeway for play and how far play can go before it hurts or interferes with the leeway of others—in which case rage is aroused or, at any rate, mimicked, and responded to with either appeasing or truly threatening gestures. In human beginnings, on the other hand, many instinctive expressions of rage and angry protest may well be an appeal for interplay: and, indeed, we see how in an infant met halfway with a playful offer anxiety and rage may at once be ameliorated. How the great human gift of *ritualization* adds structure and predictability to such vital encounters, and thus tends to make up for instinctive interplay—that we will discuss in detail in the second part. There, we will also discuss games, in childhood and beyond, as a most basic and inventive form of interplay on the border of affiliative and antagonistic interaction. But the survival value of the ritualized patterning of interplay can only become clear if we fully realize the stark probability that playfulness throughout life *is* liveliness, and that the lack of it causes a specific form of deadliness. Very early in life, an unresponsive environment is experienced as a rejecting one, just as being thwarted in one's capacity to awake interplay means to be threatened in one's being—that is, in the very rudiments of the awakening "I," and the emerging sense of "We." The first symptom of a stark lack of interplay is (as Spitz has also demonstrated) depressive withdrawal and even a lessened resistance to disease; and there is good reason to believe that in the child's unconscious the habitually unresponsive adult assumes the image of a dangerous, an iminical Other: the unresponsive eye becomes an evil one. The early experience of having one's leeway of growth curtailed, in turn, may nurture an impulsive need to coerce others by violent means, and, if this fails, as it must by the very nature of infantile impotence, a dark impulse to negate others.

If the human individual, from his ontogenetic beginnings, brings along a substratum that is best circumscribed by the words "depressive," "repressive," and "oppressive," it is once more obvious what the cultural and political setting owes each person in the way of a world view ready to confirm not only the leeway defined by what the senses learn to perceive and the skills to manage, but also a wider vision which will help overcome an always ready sense of vulnerability, impotence, and irreality. Any basic human need, however, must be viewed and reviewed in the context of those boundaries where early playfulness and the search for interplay with the Other encounters antagonistic conditions. There is the inner borderline where each human being is faced with the voice that will negate it; there is the divisive experience of selfhood which makes each being an antagonist of all others; and there is the dividing line between the "in" group, which shares a wider vision, and those "out" groups against which that vision must delineate itself by declaring them as basically dangerous and, therefore, to be ignored if distant enough, to be demeaned when too visible, and to be attacked when threatening to encroach.

All this throws much light on the beginnings of playfulness and on the end of it in various spheres of human interplay. In this connection, I would concede that some of my own formulations of adulthood call for amendment. I have in mind especially the central adult stage to which I have assigned the development of *generativity* as the human form of an instinctual drive to create and to care for new life, whether in the form of progeny, of productivity, or of creativity. My own discussion tells me that I have not sufficiently emphasized the deadliness in the development of what I have referred to as *stagnation*, the (normal or pathological) companion of generativity. For the stagnating limits of generativity in man also mark the arousal of a specific *rejectivity*, a more or less ruthless suppression or de-struction of what seems to go counter to one's "kind"—that is, the particular human subspecies or value system one wishes to propagate. This destructiveness, in the name of the highest, can express itself in moral or physical cruelty against one's children, who suddenly seem to be strangers, or against the offspring of a segment of the wider community, who appear to belong to a lower species. And this destructiveness periodically finds a vast area for collective manifestation in war or in other forms of annihilation of what suddenly appears to be a subhuman kind of man.

It will be remembered that as conservative a liberal as Walter Lippmann spoke of a pseudo-environment and, in fact, challenged the psychoanalytic claim to a normative reality. As some must have gathered, I was struck by this because I myself have attempted to circumscribe a phylogenetic phenomenon which I have named *pseudo-speciation*. Man's social evolution has built on the facts of "real" evolution a superstructure of tribal, national, and religious divisions, each dominated by a world view ascribing to itself some unquestionable superiority as "the people" and thus assigning an inferior status to all non-people. This will be discussed in greater detail presently when I proceed from the ontogenetic patterns of playfulness to phylogenetic forms of ritualization in private and in public life and will indicate how both together may help explain the life-and-death importance of human make-believe. How, indeed, is the human propensity for make-believe, which we have roughly sketched in some of its ontogenetic origins, grounded in the phylogeny of the human species; and how does such make-believe affect our sense of reality—and irreality?

Let me take up the second question first and ask whether the "natural scientist," at least, can give us a hint as to what reality is? "Einstein's final epistemological message," so Holton tells us, "was that the world of mere experience" can be explained only "in fundamental thought so general that it may be called cosmological in character." [35] At the end, it is a "leap of intuition" that divines its order. The scientific way of finding order in the cosmos is, of course, a specialization given some proven discipline and simple dignity by the continued search for *verifiable facts* and the continuing sharing and comparing of both methods and findings. The psychological root of the equally necessary search for a cosmological order, however, seems to continue that need for a world view that at a given moment of history combines obedience to verifiable new fact with a search for a *more inclusive sense of reality*, a truth held evident by a community of persons who feel that they share a living *actuality*.

All the words underlined here are, in fact, condensed in the German word *Wirklichkeit* which is either used or implied whenever Freud speaks of "reality." Factuality, then, is what at any stage of ontogeny, or at any period of science and technology, is known as verifiable and measurable. But things and facts, whether they are too simple or too complex, remain alien to us unless we recognize them as ranked within a shared world order in which each of us or, well, some chosen ones among us, have a central place —and ample leeway. *Actuality*, in turn, is the mutual actualization of individuals in the service of the facts to be mastered and of the reality to be shared and fortified; for without this double anchor in factuality and actuality, reality soon floats off into mirages and worse. Any lasting sense of truth, then, must combine the factual, the real, and the actual—and so does true playfulness. This triple anchor, however, often appears to be precariously lodged in the quicksand of human phylogeny, and this exactly where man seems divided into antagonistic political units. And if we recall that Einstein worked in a nation that fell for Hitler's mirage of a thousand years of Aryan su-

premacy, we can only conclude that the group mind any-
where is apt to harbor some more or less explicit pseudo-real
schemes which are waiting for their historical moment.

In sketching the ontogeny of playfulness, then, we are
inclined to go beyond those theories which assign legitimate play in adult life only to games or rituals taking
place in "temporary worlds within the ordinary world
dedicated to the performance of an act apart"—that is, on
toy table, playgrounds, or theatrical stages, on game boards
and sports fields, or, indeed, in high rituals reflecting a collective's mythology. No, the spirit of playfulness can pervade the visionary schemes which attach to human activities
of utter practicality and consequence, whether such
schemes are altogether implicit, or are, in fact, expressed
in terms of playful metaphors (consider, for example, the
Iron or Bamboo Curtain, or the Domino Theory) which
help to make all too convincing a sense of new complexities and help to determine, if not the initiation, at least the
general acceptance of "practical" blueprints, "strategic"
scenarios, and "objective" theories.

This is where we "came in" at the beginning of this discourse, when we quoted some experts on public opinion
expressing their shocked reaction to the general sense of
both deception and irreality in the pragmatic planning even
by the ablest and the best, who had at their disposal the
most awesome arsenal ever mobilized by a superpower.
We then set out to inquire whether the ontogeny of human imagination could help us discern how and why, in
some epochs, visionary world images inspire a distinct
sense of superior reality, with ample leeway to spare, while
in others such a vision of reality will prove to have been
fictitious, leaving the actors disoriented in mind, dispirited

in mood, and often stained with the blood of fellow men.

At any rate, it is now possible to see why it would be too simple to say that the playing child grows up to become an adult needy and ready for play only when and where reality takes time off. If childhood play seems extra-territorial to the verifiable facts and responsible acts of adult reality, it is only that playing and learning are the child's business. The adult who is playing in a sphere set aside for "play" is not comparable to a playing child; wherefore he often seems to be playing at playing. But this in no way preempts the functions of a certain maturing playfulness which is endowed with adult competence, heightens the sense of reality, and enhances actuality in spheres of activity where facts are facts and acts count. This is the lasting heritage of childhood play.

Politics at its most inspiring combines new aggregates of persons in a vision of a regenerated, a "new man" relatively adapted for the time of its ascendance to the demands of factuality and actuality. At its "dirtiest" it exploits the need for illusions and permits the study of the reciprocal collusion by which man's inner deals with himself conspire with the outer deals he is willing to acknowledge or grant to others. In the middle is the wide area (Harold Lasswell and his followers call it the relation of Idea Systems to the Self System) which demands that we study psychoanalytically how joint vision helped originate a political unit and the types of leadership peculiar to it, and the continuing meaning of the vision, the system, and the leadership for the inner life of each citizen, whatever his role in the existing hierarchies. How does a person's super-ego or ego-ideal, and how does his identity, relate dynamically to the changing world views which, as a citizen, he acknowledges or denies, exploits or falls victim to, suffers under or rebels against, cooperates with or obstructs?

These lines are often difficult to draw; but it seems that creative make-believe creates belief just because of its competence in dealing with the facts of geography and history, with ready social actualities, and with the inner lives of the people. In comparison, a certain fake reality takes over where informed and inspired vision is waning. For a while, such fake reality is eagerly held on to, even as a pervasive sense of irreality threatens. In other words, true make-believe may play with facts, but it cannot lie, while fake reality may, up to a point, seem to master the facts, but it never tells the truth.

As a further link between the ontogenetic and the phylogenetic, the individual and the institutional aspects of joint visions, it is necessary to approach a universal phenomenon on the borderline between playfulness and routinization, namely, that of everyday ritualized behavior as cultivated in all human societies in every stage of life. Once more, I must begin with the beginning, but I trust that the framework of the life cycle will provide a kind of ladder for a determined ascent to adulthood.

In the meantime, I hope to have dispelled the apprehension that I might intend to reduce politics to child's play. Reduce? May we learn to see in politics a legitimate arena of serious playfulness such as that displayed and inspired by truly great leaders.

II

Life Cycle and Ritualization

Arenas of Interplay

IN THE FIVE-YEAR-OLD'S toy construction, we saw a representation with blocks of a dancing posture adopted in the middle of school reality, even as both the toy scene and the dance step proved to be related to areas of the child's total situation—the apprehensions and impulses, the traumata and fantasies of his stage of life as well as the special problems he shared, the school he attended, and the teacher he had. Here, on the threshold from the play to the school age, we recognize both an area of play proper and an arena of interplay; and we discover a prime adaptive function of the microsphere within that larger arena. If we now would attempt to outline other stages of life, an equivalent relation of play proper to the leeway and limits of playfulness in all spheres of living, we would have to attend to what Peter Wolff has referred to as the "totality of operations" that the growing and expanding person is becoming capable of, from physical reach to cognitive comprehension, and from instinctual impulsivity to social interaction—and the limitations of these operations. In adolescence, for example, the peer generation and the ideological universe become part of the "totality of operations" even as new forms of playful activity and of games develop. To follow an individual's playfulness through life, then, would mean to chart not only what play activities are available to him, but also all forms of interplay, enveloped as they always are in a total vision of life in which a sufficient number of individuals find their private worlds confirmed. In adulthood, the work world and the procreative and productive actuality are part of the arena within which a person must have or share scope and leeway or suffer severely in his functioning. And, indeed, unless communal experiences have at each step provided the adult with a semblance of an arena of free interplay, no person can hope to reach that simple wisdom of old age when only some grasp of the wholeness of existence bounded by death can on occasion dimly recall some such promise as St. Paul's assurance that though we now look only through the "glass darkly" we will then recognize even as we will be recognized.

To follow the *forms of play* proper through the stages of life, we would have to grope our way from the infant's and the parental person's body as a source of sensation and interaction to the toy sphere of young children and to the games of older ones where political behavior is first rehearsed, as within designated spheres sides and leaders are chosen and make-believe and rules of performance agreed on. Psychosexual theory has made us acquainted with the libidinized body zones which are at children's disposal for exploratory as well as compensatory pleasure—if also for that guilt of auto-erotic interplay with oneself which can alienate the "I" from its very own body. In the toy world, it becomes significant that the child, besides finding out what things can be made to mean, also learns what proves workable in the structure of things and in the nature of basic materials; what proves permissible in imagination and acceptable in the social world of playmates; and, in fact, what will be sanctioned by adult guardians. To follow such different forms of play through childhood and youth, then, would also mean to indicate how spheres of play and how games increasingly reach into the arena of responsible and irreversible action, the microsphere of play table and sports field into the macrosphere of "political" conflict. In youth, as we have seen in recent decades so dramatically and some-times tragically, the delineation of prank from criminal deed, and of playacting from political act, is often difficult; and nowhere, as we have learned, is it more important to open up new arenas of competent and thoughtful interplay than in the interaction of technological youth and the widening arena of its political awareness.

In repeating "this we would have to do," I mean to say, of course, that I will not even try to do this here, for nothing short of a textbook or a survey of existing textbooks could accomplish this task. So I will chart only one use of play-fulness throughout life which has received little attention, namely, what I call ritualization in everyday life.

But before I leave the spatial aspects of play, I must say a word about games as the most social and sociable use of a bounded play space in which the players in playing their assigned roles to perfection seem to become themselves the toys of fate. Mutual interplay, as we saw, is governed by the eagerness and the capacity of persons to enhance each other's leeway in affiliative and erotic ways. But as each expands in his readinesses, he also persistently experiences the boundaries where *reciprocal antagonisms* set one person against another and one group against others. It is this dividing line which, it seems, is dramatized and formalized from childhood on, in games which gradually turn into full-grown sports. Here again, a circumscribed area is marked off as a proving ground, a field with magic meanings clearly defined for participant and onlooker. Teams of antagonists become engaged—and "engagement" is the word for interplay *and* for combat—on the two sides of a clearly marked dividing line. How thus playfulness becomes gamesmanship is one of the most fascinating chapters in the animal as well as the human world.

Here I can only refer to the comprehensive work of Sutton-Smith, who analyzes the "social structure" of the games of children as encounters in a special "space-time scene": hide-and-seek, chase and escape, capture and rescue, seduction and harassment. Whether the outcome of such games depends on skill, chance, or strategy, they reflect not only the cognitive and physical capacities of given age groups, but also "models of power, by which we mean that they are buffered learning situations through which the child gains acquaintance and experience at the power stratagems relevant to some of the major parameters of influence within his own culture." [1]

Referring to Lévi-Strauss's work, Sutton-Smith calls games "a form of war which can occur only amongst those who are at peace." In the context of this book, I can only attempt to sketch the common structure of games (as compared to that, already sketched, of toy scenes) as a further bridge between the individual ego's space-time and a society's world view.

From the most childlike gameliness (I'll bite you if you bite me, but I won't hurt you much if you don't hurt me much) to the traditional scenarios of children's games all the way to the international sports arena, each player is allotted a strategic position on one or the other side of an imaginary or real line crossing an arena dominated by magic "rules of the game." Here again, the ontogenetic development of playfulness into sportsmanship makes it possible to train in the human being what can only be called a nonviolent discipline which is already instinctively given in the games of higher animals. An "equivalent to war," indeed.

What is phylogenetic in this ontogeny? Gregory Bateson has described animal interplay under the title, "This Is Play"—meaning that animals are instinctively intent on signaling each other when pseudo-antagonistic actions are to be taken as an invitation to play. Eibl-Eibesfeldt [2] reports that in the playful acts of some animals even action patterns otherwise belonging to separate spheres of instinctive behaviors programmed for good phylogenetic reasons to exclude each other—such as hunting, fighting, and mating—can appear side by side in special combinations without being consummated in the catch, the kill, or the act of mating.

In the human species, institutionalized games take place bounded in a special space and a programmed time. A set number of participants is divided into opposite but equal teams, each distinguished by insignia and often also a magic name. This field may be surrounded by viewers—themselves divided in their team sympathies. The game as a test of loyalty, skill, and fate is decided in favor of one team, while the other is guaranteed another chance. Thus, each side, while highly committed in its loyalties, remains exchangeably identified with the opponent who is expert in the same sport, accepts the same rules, is subject to the same fate, and thus, in principle, takes an equal chance. Furthermore, each player, on either side, must have learned to adapt himself, at least while he plays, to a gamesmanship combining passion and restraint, discipline and originality—all of which promises to make the best players charismatic symbols of the new man in a new team in a new season. In such game reality, symbolic acts can be committed, symbolic emotions experienced, and alternations of symbolic doom and triumph accepted which in "real life" might mean the absolute dominance or total defeat of one or the other side, with all the inhumanities and reality distortions attending the reciprocity of mortal enmity among different species. It is in gamesmanship that man is most human in the sense of an acceptance of his adversary as equally human: as one side enjoys unambiguous victory without usurpation, and clear-cut defeat without annihilation, an equilibrium of skill and chance is maintained. Probably the closest parallel to this in politics is the nonviolent technique advocated and experimented with by Gandhi and sporadically so appealing to groups seeking a reconciliation of religious and political propensities in mankind.[3]

Games stand midway between individual play in the toy world and the arena of politics in which human beings unite in communal interplay and establish rules for joining and for contesting with each other. Each such polis, too, is governed by a shared vision according to which a preordained type of man enjoys a maximum of individual leeway (now called freedom) within a legalized system of traditional antagonisms. As to the antagonisms between any given polis and a substratum of its own population or between neighboring political areas, there still seem to exist, up to a point, "rules of warfare" and styles of combat in theaters of war. Not only in complex "war games," but also in the very conduct of war itself, a kind of gamesmanship called military reaches into the very front-line engagement of groups of men, decked out by a display of plumage marking a special kind of specieshood, and inspired by special leaders to conduct specified kinds of mutual annihilation under honorable conditions and for some higher glory. All this has, of course, been eroded by mechanization, from the gun to the bomb, and it is only the *homo novus* of technocratic society who can coldly plan for and speak of "overkill": we will come to that. For that very reason, the idea of nonviolence—and the devotional frames of mind that would support it—has taken hold as one promising guarantor of survival.

At any rate, any ontogenetic reconstruction of the relation of play to politics would have to begin with the meaning of ritualized interplay for the development of the individual ego, and would have to proceed from the political element in games to the game element in political action.

Speciation and Ritualization

AT THE CONCLUSION of the first part, I suggested that it may be the very condition of pseudo-speciation which has made man's playfulness a matter both of freedom and of bondage, both of increased actuality and of confounded irreality, both of enhanced life and of multiplied death. For in league with mankind's most archaic heritage, namely, the fateful interrelation of self-hate and the hate of otherness, pseudo-speciation has dominated man's history to the present, the nuclear, day. Let me emphasize here, however, that I do not say that either mankind as a whole, or any part of it, *is* a "pseudo-species." I do submit that human specieshood has a built-in tendency toward pseudo-speciation, which, under certain conditions, makes sections of it act as if they were separate species.

But what do we mean by "pseudo"? This can be an angry

word, where it alludes to fake or malicious deception. The more descriptive naturalistic meaning merely assigns to the appearance of something a convincing similarity to something else which it isn't. In human make-believe, in turn, one must think of a whole range of images and behaviors from genuine role playing and creative pretense to intentional and political deception. The human condition is confounded by the fact that we must learn, as we grow up, to adapt the workings of our unconscious and the topology of our inner conflicts to the imagery and the language of our "kind" which is defined by its place in geography and history as well as by its stage of culture and technology. For since, according to Ernst Mayr, we are the "generalist animal," we are born with the potential of growing into one of a vast variety of natural environments and cultural settings. Our "subspecies," being technically and culturally adapted to a given environment, must make unique sense not only in terms of production and consumption, but also of fate and existence, and must permit its dominant type (its *homo novus*, its Adam) to act as if it were *the* human being, central to and in the universe. History, of course, has alternately counterpointed and yet also reconciled such difference (within empires and religions) and has thereby created more inclusive human identities—a process which has led to some sense of one future specieshood.

By pseudo-speciation, then, we mean a sense of irreversible difference between one's own and other "kinds," which can attach itself to evolved major differences among human populations or, indeed, to smaller and smallest differences which have come to loom large. In the form of man's "in"-group loyalties, such a specific sense of being elect—as a tribe or nation, creed, class, or ideology—can contribute to the highest achievements in citizenship, courage, and workmanship and can, in fact, weld together in new loyalties (*civis Romanus*, Christian love) previously inimical entities. In the form of new "out"-group enmities, on the other hand, it can express itself most variably—in mortal hatred as well as in phobic avoidance, or in sheer clannishness. Such prejudice may make men more beastly than any beasts could be, or it may, under peaceful conditions, make men vie with each other for the right vision—or countervision—within agreed-upon procedures. Most important, the remnants of pseudo-speciation permit historical circumstances to bring about abrupt and intense changes in all these forms; while, in the meantime, the ritualizations of everyday life to be described here continue to depend on a strong sense of what is appropriate and essential to one's sanctioned kind.

Here, then, is the phylogenetic crux of the specifically human problem of make-believe and reality. The generalist aspects of its endowment have given mankind a highly flexible drive equipment ("instinctual," in Freud's sense) instead of the animal's "instinctive" adaptation to a limited environment which, as long as it does not change catastrophically, confirms a species by the fit of inborn pattern and material fact. In mankind, the very capacity for creative imagination must make up for a certain unreliability of instinctual equipment and the variability of culture artifacts. Psychoanalysis, in fact, usually assigns to instinctual drives the connotation of a quantitative excess potentially dangerous to the parsimony of specific patterns of "fittedness." The evolutionary rationale for this free-floating quantity of instinctual energy lies, of course, in the very fact that man is born to invest relatively nonspecific drives in such interplay as will assure, during a long childhood, the necessary combination of mutuality, competence, and identity. The growing child's play (and that is what a long childhood is for) is the training ground for the experience of a leeway of imaginative choices within an existence governed and guided by roles and visions. These, however, must undergo meaningful adjustments during economic and historical upheavals, wherefore man must suffer (and that is what adolescence is for) a certain identity confusion during which the adolescing person may be glad to accept existing confirmations or feel creatively moved, ideologically inspired—or, indeed, motivated to destroy.

We will come back to adolescence—and to rites. In the following, however, I would like to differentiate between special rituals and rites, on the one hand, and the *ritualized customs* of everyday life which first formalize human playfulness and ally it to a special seriousness.[4] In passing, I should note that the words "ritual" and "ritualization" mean different things in different fields and can have the best and the worst of connotations. When in psychopathology we speak of an individual's "handwashing ritual," we mean that he scrubs his hands, in tortured solitude, until they become raw, and yet he never feels clean. But this blatantly contradicts the anthropological meaning of the word, which assigns to "ritual" a deepened communality, a proven ceremonial form, and a timeless quality from which all participants emerge with a sense of awe and purification.

Ethologists have followed up Julian Huxley's suggestion that the word "ritualization" be used for such phylogenetically preformed ceremonial acts as, for example, the dramatic greeting ceremony displayed by pairs of penguins at the time when the males return from their long expeditions beyond the seas: they thereby confirm their own identities and the identity of their mates and their offspring, who had awaited them in the one right nest among the vast multitude of nests in a crowded colony. Such ritualized interplay, here "instinctive," is the affirmation of a bond in the form of a reciprocal message of supreme adaptive importance. When asked to consider what comparable phenomena in human life might be called "ritualizations," I first had to separate the grand display of rituals and periodic ceremonies from the formalization of minute patterns of daily interplay. In this last sense, ritualization is a mixture of formality and improvisation, a rhyming in time. It is closer to a *ritus* as a daily custom than to a rite as a periodical ceremony; although daily custom creates ritual needs which then find periodical fulfillment in grand rituals. But the various terms for ritual displays have in common etymological origins and usages which, so I concluded, are best expressed with *measured in space and time*, and also apply to a carefully dosed and playfully repeated item of daily custom—beginning, I will submit, with the way we welcome a newborn.

It is only a seeming paradox that newly born Man, who could, in principle and probably within some genetic limits, fit into any number of pseudo-species and their habitats, must for that very reason be coaxed and induced to become "speciated" during a prolonged childhood by some form of family: he must be *familiarized by ritualization* with a particular version of human existence. He thus develops a distinct sense of corporate identity, later fortified against the encroachment of other pseudo-species by prejudices which can make very small differences in ritualization extraspecific and, in fact, inimical to the only "genuine" human identity.

Let me link the subjects of world view and ritualization with an anthropological bit of information first related in *Childhood and Society;*[5] for we must realize from the outset that ritualization is an aspect of everyday life which is more clearly seen in a different culture or class or even family than in our own, where, in fact, ritualization is more often than not experienced simply as the only proper way to do things; and the question is only why does not everybody do it our way. I share, I am sure, with all anthropologists (professional and amateur) the wonder with which one encounters in the field old people who will tenderly describe what once was appropriate in their culture, displaying a sense of moral and aesthetic rightness in details unquestionably sanctioned by the universe. Here is what Fanny, the Yurok shaman, told me of the right way to conduct an ordinary meal, among the Yurok Indians in northern California, who depended on the salmon and its elusive ways (long hidden to science) of propagating and migrating. A strict order of placement was maintained. A child old enough to "have sense" was taught to eat in prescribed ways. The child was to put only a little food on the spoon, to take the spoon up to his mouth slowly, to put the spoon down again while chewing the food—and, above all, to think of becoming rich while he enjoyed and swallowed it. Everybody was silent during meals, so that all could keep their thoughts concentrated on shell money and salmon. Such ritualization lifted to the level of a kind of oral hallucination certain nostalgic needs which were cultivated throughout life and ceremonially intensified under ritual conditions.

What we have observed above about eating and seeing, hoping and believing, at the very beginning of life, gives such ritualization a good ontogenetic base, except that at what primitive cultures call the "sense" stage, the child can be expected to begin to grasp the symbolic meaning of behavior and accept both restriction and delay for the sake of cultural belongingness within a world view of cosmic magic. Later, in the men's "sweat house," the adolescing boy would learn the dual feat of thinking of money and *not* thinking of women; and the adult Yurok could make himself see money hanging from trees and salmon swimming in the river during the off season in the belief that this self-induced "hallucinatory" thought would melt the hearts of the Providers beyond the ocean who had the power to detain the year's supply of salmon there or generously send it during the yearly salmon run up the mouths of the rivers and, with an overwhelming onrush, right into the nets and dams of waiting humanity.

There is much about Yurok "culture and personality" (terms which once dominated such investigations) which could be called "compulsive" and compared with the "rituals" of neurotics in our culture. But as I pointed out in *Childhood and Society*, such behavior made sense as a ritualized attempt to influence magically the well-observed but, of course, not understood complexities of the salmon's natural history. And ritualization in our sense is anything but neurotic symptomatology where it supports the formation of a set of behavior patterns combining human propensities in a cultural system within a circumscribed section of nature and technology. Thus daily ritualization can serve as adaptive interplay deemed central to both the natural and the social universe. That this, no doubt, in daily usage is apt to develop into an orthodoxy of mere social compulsion and compliance subject to "deals" which sacrifice the spirit to the letter—that is a matter of social pathology to be discussed later.

Ritualization at its best, that is, in a viable cultural setting, represents a *creative formalization* which helps to avoid both *impulsive* excess and *compulsive* self-restriction, both social anomie and moralistic coercion. It thus, I will now claim, accomplishes a formidable number of things:

1. It elevates the satisfaction of immediate needs (here, hunger) into the context of a communal actuality. It therefore offers some instinctuality for sublimation (tamed eagerness) while it firmly joins the as yet vulnerable sense of personal (ego) centrality to a group's idea of its central place in the natural and spiritual universe.

2. In teaching a sanctioned way of doing simple and daily things, it transforms the infantile sense of omnipotence into a joint sense of manifest destiny (power over the salmon's mysterious life cycle).

3. It deflects feelings of unworthiness onto outsiders within and without one's culture who are excluded or exclude themselves from knowing the right way.

4. It puts emerging cognitive patterns in the service of a general vision shared by the community: in the example of the Yurok meal, I would presume, ritualization not only makes use of what has been learned in a sensory-motor way in the feeding experience and in the earliest encounter with reliably existing providers, it also uses and cultivates the

growing cognitive capacity to discern what distinguishes the right class of things and people from the wrong one.

5. As it will be our particular intention to indicate, in each successive stage ritualization helps develop essential aspects of all ritual sense (here, the sacramental meaning of the oral intake of sacrificial bodies), which later on will be found to be an outstanding element in the inventory of adult ritual.

6. It develops the experience of a social differentiation essential to one of the major institutions of any functioning society—here, the discrimination between prescribed and good behavior and shameful or guilty acts which in adulthood are encountered in judicial contexts.

7. And, finally, it provides the psychosocial foundation for the gradual development of an independent identity to be sealed in adolescence by various rituals of "confirmation"—a "second birth" which will integrate all childhood identifications in a world view and belief system while marking as ideologically foreign all those wishes and images which have become undesirable and evil and are remindful of other, "lower" species of men.

All this said, it must be clear that we would expect ritualization to be a major link between the ego's propensity for orientation in space and time and the world views dominating (or competing in) a society. In psychopathology, however, we can (and should) study the way ritualized schemes of behavior have fallen apart, isolating persons and their lonely conflicts. We may then offer therapeutic ritualizations which provide new insights into human adaptation. But only in the study of "live" ritualization in everyday life can we learn how persons and conflicts find a mutual fit in generational patterns, or how, indeed, the lack of true ritualization or its decline into false ritualism can lead to social pathology.

Such insights, it seems, might be particularly important in periods of rapid change, where ritualization (of a more punitive, say, or a more permissive kind, or of a different assignment of sex roles) disintegrates under the impact of changing ideology and technology. New ritualizations, however, emerge only where some dominant ethos emerges in consonance with new material facts, a new sense of reality, and new incentives for interplay in actuality.

Ritualization in Everyday Life

LET US BEGIN, then, with the way the maternal person and the infant greet each other in the morning. The awakening infant awakens in the maternal person a whole repertoire of emotive, verbal, and manipulative behavior. She approaches him with smiling or worried concern, brightly or anxiously voicing some appellation, and goes into action: looking, feeling, sniffing, she discovers possible sources of discomfort and initiates services to be rendered by rearranging the infant's position, by picking him up, and so on. This daily event is highly ritualized, in that the mother seems to feel obliged, and not a little pleased, to repeat a performance arousing in the infant predictable responses, which, in turn, encourage her to proceed. Such ritualization is at the same time highly individual ("typical" for the particular mother and also tuned to the particular infant) and yet also stereotyped along some traditional lines subject to anthropological description. It is more or less freely given and responded to, and more or less coerced by duty. The whole procedure is superimposed on the periodicity of physical needs close to the requirements of survival; it is also an emotional necessity in the generational process; and it counts on the child's growing cognitive capacity and eagerness. In fact, while I will not make a point of it, I trust that the stages of ritualization to be proposed here are in line with the established lawfulness of Piaget's stages—except that, to begin with, one would have to assume an observational situation in which the observer charts not only the infant's sensory-motor interaction with the "environment," but also the mother's interplay with the infant's cognitive search—and the interplay of both with the observer.

Our point is that this bit of playful routine can be properly evaluated only as a small but tough link in the whole formidable sequence of generations. As mother and infant meet in the first ritualization described so far, the infant brings to the constellation his vital needs (among "instinctual" drives subsumed as oral, sensory, and tactile in libido theory) and the necessity to have disparate experiences made coherent by mothering. The mother in her postpartum state is also needful in a complex manner: for whatever instinctive sense of mothering she may be endowed with, and whatever instinctual gratification she may seek in being a mother, she also needs to become a mother of a special kind and in a special way. This she becomes by no means without an anxious avoidance (sometimes phobic, often superstitious) as well as some more or less subdued anger over the coerciveness of routine and role. Along with the positive image of a mothering received by and watched in people of her own kind, there are elements of a negative identity, namely, what she must not do or be lest she resemble "other" kinds and ways typical for persons or groups whom she (more or less consciously) dislikes or despises, hates, or fears as godless or evil, unhygienic or immoral—or guided by images of womanhood protested by her. Luckily, the mother is affirmed in her new role by identification with those who mothered her well; while her own motherhood is reaffirmed as benevolent by the increasing responsiveness of the infant. The infant, in turn, develops a benevolent self-image (a certified narcissism, we may say) grounded in the recognition of an all-powerful and mostly benevolent (if sometimes strangely malevolent) Other. While the mother's postpartum condition enhances this interplay, it is clear that sooner or later any truly maternal person can replace the "birth mother."

Let us take the fact that the mother calls the infant by a name. This may have been carefully selected and perhaps certified in some name-giving ritual, held to be indispensable by the parents and the community. Yet, whatever procedures have given meaning to the name, that meaning now exerts a certain effect on the way in which the name is repeated during the greeting procedure—together with other emphases of caring attention which have a very special meaning for the maternal person(s) and eventually for the child. Thus, the mother also refers to herself with a special designation. This mutual assignment of a very special meaning is, I think, the ontogenetic source of one pervasive element in human ritualization, which is based on a *mutuality of recognition*, by face and by name.

There is much to suggest that man is born with the need for such regular and mutual affirmation and certification: we know at any rate that its absence can harm an infant radically, by diminishing or extinguishing his search for impressions which will verify his senses. This need will reassert itself in every stage of life as a demand for ever new, ever more formalized and more widely shared ritualizations (and, eventually, rituals) which repeat the face-to-face "recognition" and the name-to-name correspondence of the hoped for. Such ritualizations range from the regular exchange of greetings affirming a strong emotional bond, to traditional greetings affirming a reciprocity of roles, to singular encounters in love or inspiration, and, eventually, in a leader's "charisma" as confirmed by (more or less) exquisite statues and paintings, or by mere multiplied banners and televised appearances. All such meetings at their best embody seeming paradoxes: they are *playful* and yet *formalized;* quite *familiar* through repetition, they yet renew the *surprise* of recognition. And while the ethologists will tell us that ritualizations in the animal world must, above all, be *unambiguous* sets of signals which avoid the arousal of conflicting instinctive patterns, we suspect that in man the overcoming of *ambivalence* (as well as of ambiguity) is one of the prime functions of ritualization. For as we love our children, and children in general, they can also arouse hate and murderous disdain, even as at best they will find us arbitrary in rejection and possessive in acceptance, if not potentially dangerous and witchlike. What we love or admire is always also threatening; awe becomes awfulness, and benevolence harbors the danger of being consumed by wrath. Therefore, ritualized affirmation, reaching from daily life to religious rites, becomes indispensable as a periodical experience and must in changing times find new and meaningful forms.

This is a heavy burden to place on an infant's daily awakening, and, indeed, only the whole sequence of stages of ritualization can make this list of essentials plausible. Yet psychopathology confirms this early burdening. Of all psychological disturbances which we have learned to connect ontogenetically with the early stages of life, the deepest and most devastating (as Spitz and Bowlby have shown) are those in which the light of mutual recognition and of hope is early forfeited in autistic and psychotic withdrawal. For the earliest affirmation soon becomes much needed reaffirmation in the face of the fact that the very experiences which through ritualization give a measure of security also expose the growing being to a *series of estrangements:* these, too, we must try to specify as we deal with each developmental stage. In the first stage, I submit, it is a sense of *separation* and *abandonment* which is never quite overcome by periodical reassurance of familiarity and mutuality; while this first and dimmest affirmation, this sense of a hallowed presence, contributes to mankind's ritual-making a pervasive element which is best called the *numinous.* This designation betrays my intention to follow the earliest into the last: and, indeed, we recognize the numinous as an indispensable aspect of the devotional element in all periodical observances. However, it must be clear that of all institutions that of organized religion has the strongest claim to being in charge of the numinous: the believer, by appropriate gestures, confesses his dependence and his childlike faith and seeks, by appropriate offerings, to secure the privilege of being lifted up to the very bosom of the divine which, indeed, may be seen to graciously respond, with the faint smile of an inclined face. The numinous assures us of *separateness transcended* and yet also a *distinctiveness confirmed*, and thus of the very basis of a sense of "I," renewed (as it feels) by the mutual recognition of all "I"s joined in a shared faith in one all-embracing "I Am."

As we proceed through ontogeny, however, let us be aware also of those deceptive and self-deceptive trends which are the shadow of all make-believe and of playful ritualization. I will attempt to name for each stage one element of that pervasive social pathology by which ritualization in its "measured" relation to over-all reality (in the three meanings discussed) is perverted into what could be called pseudo-ritualization, or more simply, *ritualism*. This takes many forms, from mere compulsive compliance with daily rules to the obsessive-repetitive expression of fanatic and delusional visions. The first of these ritualisms may be called *idolism*, which distorts the reverence for the truly numinous. Such an "ism," of course, often fits in with prevailing character types and with important social trends and yet is apt to lose its playful relation to both fact and principle and become habitual and obsessive. The numinous thus can be lost in adulation—an attitude falling short (and this is the main point) of the psychosocial and generational integration inherent in a true sense of veneration or even adoration. The illusory image of perfection—including that of the self-image—implied in the relation of idolizer and idol is, of course, distorted by an excess in that libidinal attachment to the self which we call narcissism, after the mythical young man who perished rather than abandon his (and with his, a dead twin sister's) face reflected in a mountain pool: a double mirroring, then, instead of a commitment to a living love.

If, again, I have dwelt unduly long on the first stage, I have also declared my principles of presentation. But there remains one question which we must ask about each element of ritualization: as it survives in and grows with the growing person, what does it contribute to and what does it demand of the community's vision? Here we must underline once more the changing fields of vision successively experienced in the process of growing up from a supine newborn to the kind of upright creature we are.

Man's inner structure, we said, has evolved together with his institutions. The human being which at the beginning wants, in addition to the fulfillment of oral and sensory needs, to be gazed upon by the primal parent and to respond to the gaze, to look up to the parental countenance and to be responded to, continues to look up, and to look for somebody to look up to, and that is somebody who will, in the very act of returning his glance, lift him up. It is clear that the religious element in any collective vision responds to this first stage. In the Visconti Hours, where Barbello depicts Maria's death, God in heaven is shown holding in his arms her spirit in the form of a swaddled baby, and "returning the gaze of Mary's soul." This closes the cycle of the first stage as projected on the whole of existence. In religion, vision becomes Revelation, and revelatory spectacles, all confirming the immortality of the "I," if also under strict rules and often awful threats of total abandonment. Now, each religion has its own political structure; and politics proper always competes with religion (joining it, tolerating it when it must, and absorbing it when it can) in order to promise, if not a life beyond, then a new deal on this earth, and a Leader smiling charismatically from the placards. Yet, in any true ritual as well as in any working combination of all ritualizations, this one element tends to be integrated with all others.

CHILDHOOD AND THE JUDICIOUS: THE WORD AND THE LAW

A second basic element in human ritualization is one for which the best term would seem to be "judicious" because it combines *jus* and *dicere*, "the law" and "the word." We saw in the Yurok's ritualization of the daily meal an example of a method of behavior, no doubt suggested in approving and disapproving words and tone of voice, by which the *discrimination* between right and wrong or clean and unclean is ontologically established and ready to relate to law outside as well as to the voice of conscience within. Eventually, this becomes an essential aspect in all human ritual; for there is no ritual—up to the Last Judgment—which does not imply a severe discrimination between the sanctioned and the out-of-bounds.

The ontological source of this second kind of ritualization is the second stage of life, characterized as it is by rapid advances in psychosocial *autonomy*. As the ability to crawl and eventually to stand serves increased self-reliance, it also soon leads to play with the boundaries of the permissible. If, to the first stage, namely, infancy, I have ascribed the rudiments of *hope*, I consider *will* to be the basic strength founded in the second stage, that is, early childhood. The new acquisitions in cognitive as well as in muscular and locomotor capacities and the increased readiness for interplay with others fosters, under favorable conditions, a great pleasure in exerting one's will and in being found both capable of and justified in using it. This, then, is the ontogenetic origin of that great human preoccupation with a "free will" which will look for and find its test in the ritualization in daily life of matching judgments as to what constitutes arenas for self-assertion. Yet, to stand upright means to be looked at from all sides, even from behind, the area of ourselves hidden to ourselves. The very autonomy gained in the second stage, namely, a sense of being a separate person with a will born of self-will and tamed primarily by self-control—that autonomy soon finds its limits in our sensitive awareness of being watched by superior persons and of being called names, even bestial ones. Worse, we are shamable, and we blush for all to see. To learn to avoid being laughed at, then, means to learn to look at ourselves and our acts from outside and to adjust our will to the views of those who judge us. But this also demands the development of that inner self-watch which Freud called the super-ego, that is, literally a part of ourselves standing watch over the rest of ourselves and confronting us with detestable self-images. We thus learn to look down upon ourselves as unworthy and guilty, and are apt to do so with such cruelty that we sometimes feel relieved only when punished. Nor could we face ourselves did we not also learn to look down on others as we look down on creeping creatures. We can then protest we are not the lowest, and can claim that we belong to the relatively elect. This is one ontogenetic contribution of this stage to shared visions. In the meantime, ritualized ways of playfully testing these limits by an interplay of daring deeds on the child's part and of loud praise or mocking disdain on the part of older children or adults establish what "looks right" or "does not look right" in the eyes of others; while the development of word meanings (obviously, one of the very strongest bonds of pseudo-species)

attaches finite classifications dominated by "Yes" and "No"
to what is conceptually integrated in the verbalized world,
and what remains outside, nameless, unmeaningful, strange,
foreign, *wrong*. All of this can be given strong connotations by psychosexual "anality," the instinctual endowment
with special pleasure of the zones serving the eliminative
and retentive modes. What at first is experienced as a
warm possession must yet be eliminated well and in the right
way and in the right place as symbolical of all that (people
say) smells bad, is dirty, and may be poisonous. But this
estranges the child from its own back- and underside—and,
indeed, standing upright with an exposed backside invisible to himself, the child realizes that he can lose face
and suffer a shaming which, at its worst, uses excremental
designations along with references to lower creatures. Giving himself away by blushing, he can feel furiously isolated, not knowing whether to doubt himself or all those
who judge. His elders, in turn, feel compelled to utilize
and thus to aggravate this division; and yet, is it not again
in the ritualization of approval and disapproval (in recur-
ring situations of high symbolic meaning) that the adult
speaks as a judicial mouthpiece of a communal righteousness, damning the deed, but giving another chance to the
doer?

This second element of ritualization is differentiated
from the first primarily by an emphasis on the assumption
of an ever freer will to make the right choices. In the ritualization of infancy, avoidances were the parents' responsibility; now the child himself is trained to "watch himself." To
this end, parents and other elders compare him (to his
face) with what he might become if he (and they) did not
watch out, thus creating two opposite images of himself.

Here, then, is the ontogenetic source of the "negative identity" which is so essential in the imagery supporting pseudospeciation, for it embodies everything one is *not* supposed to be or show—and what one yet feels one potentially is. And, indeed, slang language uses explicit images and names referring to animal species and lower human pseudospecies which one must *not* resemble in order to have a chance of acceptance in one's own. Behind the dreaded traits, of course, are often images of what the parents themselves had been tempted to become and therefore doubly fear the child might turn out to be—*potential* traits, then, which the child yet must learn to imagine in order to be able to avoid them. The self-doubt and the hidden shame attached to the necessity of "eliminating" part of himself create in the human being a certain subdued rage which eventually must either rebel against the condemning authority or turn righteous condemnation against others. I paint this matter darkly because here we meet the ontological origin not only of the *divided self* but also that of the *divided species*. For there is no doubt that unbearable prejudice against the self is at the bottom of much of the human proclivity for compulsive, obsessive, and depressive disorders; while irrational prejudice against other kinds, armed with modern weapons, may yet make for the reciprocal annihilation of pseudo-species, perhaps on the verge of becoming one real one. All of this, however, underscores the constant need for new everyday ritualizations of moral discrimination in words and sounds truly corresponding to a shared moral climate which the child can comprehend—and experiment with.

It is not difficult to see what adult ritual is rooted in this phase of life. In its full elaboration in the spectacle of a *trial* this judicious element is reaffirmed on a grand scale, making all-visible on the public stage a drama that is familiar to each individual's inner life—for the law, we must be made to believe, is untiringly watchful as is, alas, our conscience. The principle of it all, written into our belief system as it is ossified in the lawbooks, is fulfilled where law enforcement delivers a suitable culprit. Once in the dock, he serves as "an example," on which a multitude can project their inner shame, as his deeds are made to parade past the parental judge, the fraternal jury, and the chorus of the public. Judgment is pronounced as based on sanctified agreement rather than on passing outrage or personal revenge; and whether or not the culprit accepts the punishment with repentance, and whether or not the punishment will, indeed, "teach him a lesson," justice has been served.

Throughout life, the everyday establishment of boundaries of good or bad and of clean and unclean as they culminate in the judiciary ritual in the adult world fulfill the criteria for all rituals: meaningful regularity; ceremonial attention to detail and to the total procedure; a symbolic sense surpassing the reality of each participant and of the deed itself; a mutual activation of all concerned (including, or so it is hoped, the confessing culprit); and a sense of absolute indispensability. For the judicious element, too, is an intrinsic aspect of man's phylogenetic adaptation as well as his ontogenetic development.

In seeing the judicious factor at work, however, in public and in private, we can also perceive where this form of ritualization can fail in its adaptive function: in the convincing transmission of bearable and workable boundaries from generation to generation. The judicial ritual at large, with its task of establishing objective *legal* guilt as a threatening example to potential culprits, is all too often too far removed from the subjective processes which make a person feel *morally* liable. The judicial system actually can feed on the morally unreliable, for it tends to emphasize fearful compulsion to conform rather than free assent to what feels right; it can emphasize the obsessively formalistic and bureaucratic over the convincingly ceremonial; while with its display it may feed sensational voyeurism, and in its penal procedures, moralistic sadism. All of this increases the hopeless isolation of the culprit and can aggravate an impotent rage which will only make him more "shameless." Thus, the second great element of ritualism comes to the fore, which we may call *legalism:* the victory of the letter over the spirit of the word and the law. It is expressed in the vain display of righteousness or empty contrition, or in a moralistic insistence on exposing and isolating the culprit whether or not this will be good for him or anybody else. All this concerns the inner deals which human beings make with their own sense of righteousness and shame, and the "political" deals made possible by the legalistic mechanisms of justice. Here again, the psychopathology attending the failure of everyday ritualization and the social pathology characterizing the malfunctioning of ritual institutions are closely related. As ritualization fails to prevent the alternation of shameless impulsivity and meticulous compulsivity, of excess and of self-restriction in individuals, so the institution can fail to stem either widespread lawlessness or a punitive miscarriage of justice.

We may pause to summarize at this point that according to *epigenetic* development each element of ritualization which later becomes the core of a major human institution is rooted in a distinct stage of childhood, but is absorbed by and renewed in all subsequent ones. Thus, the numinous element reappears in the judicial ritualization as the aura adhering to all just authority, and is later recognized in images of divine or secular justice; or in concrete individuals who as justices are invested with the personified power of that image; or in the moral classification of "the just." But this also means that neither the numinous nor the judicious factors, although they are each inherent in a particular stage in childhood and come to be the essence of a particular institution in adulthood, can "make up" a true ritual by themselves: all the later elements as yet to develop must join them. Of these, I will discuss in the following the elements of *dramatic elaboration*, which brings us back to childhood play; of *formal competence*, the goal of the school age; and of *ideological commitment*, the task of youth.

PLAY AGE AND THE DRAMATIC: THE ACT AND THE IMAGE

First, then, the *dramatic* element. We need to remind ourselves only of a few of the themes of the play constructions mentioned to understand that drama is grounded in the maturational advances of the *play age* which permit the child to create with available objects a *coherent plot with conflicting turns* and some form of resolution. It will be remembered that the boy's block construction suggested an erect body, arms outstretched—dancing. Yet it was the black boy doll which seemed to be the figure closest to the play-constructing boy himself in sex, age, and race, and which, although supine, occupied the highest place in the construction. He was, we surmised, the *hero* of a conflict which we could recognize only in its thematic outline but could not fully interpret in its personal meaning. Yet the boy's brief story pointed to a villain, the snake, condemned to permanent existence on the ground, and thus symbolizing lowness as well as sneaky danger; with the somewhat higher animals delegated to subdue and to destroy it. Are the people with their arms spread out excited and, maybe, elated over the defeat of evil, which they are witnessing?

If the towering block construction represents some kind of victory, however, it cannot escape us that it also resembles a cross, a holy symbol. We see how infinitely far a few simple themes could carry us—too far, some will say with a shudder—and yet, while we should not presume to be sure of any of our interpretations without being able to pursue them into the details of the playing child's life or to compare a single construction with many others, neither should we refrain from attending to the thematic suggestions offered so we may discern their configurational logic —here, for example, the spatial logic of such pairs of meaning as high up and lowdown, dancing and crawling, erect and supine, on top and underneath. All of this, seen together with such temporal dimensions as doom and promise, seems to give a shared meaning to some central conflict which could lead us from his boy's construction to some of the mightiest themes of myth and drama.

As for the play stage proper, we recognize in many play constructions what we have come to formulate as the psychosocial problem of *initiative*. The play age, we said, offers the child a micro-reality in which he can use toys (put at his disposal by those who sanction his play) in order to relive, correct, and re-create past experiences, and anticipate future roles and events with the spontaneity and repetitiveness which characterize all creative ritualization. The play themes of this age, however, often prove to be dominated by the usurpation and ambitious impersonation of victorious self-images and the killing off of weak and evil "others"; and we nominate for the principal inner estrangement which finds expression, aggravation, or resolution in childhood play the *sense of guilt*. Thus, the playing child, in initiating a toy scene, often can be seen to play out the question of what range of activity is open to him and what direction will engulf him in guilt.

One might think that any sense of guilt should be subsumed under the themes of the judicial sphere. But a culprit, by definition, has failed to be guided by conscience; for this very reason he must be exposed publicly by those who will shame him at least into the admission of what has become evident, which may make him legally guilty but by no means assures that he feels really responsible and personally guilty. A true sense of guilt stems from a *self*-condemnation so inescapable that it might not even wait for the fantasied deed to be actually committed; or if committed in secret, to be known to others; or if known to others, to be punished by them. It is, in fact, through the inescapability of inner guilt as expressed in play that the *dramatic element* first enters ontogeny. But where, one may ask, is the interplay in solitary play? Our example is taken from a very special situation, a planned procedure testing a child's imagination with toys selected by us for their suggestive value and in a protected setting. But so must a child in everyday life use a given toy world, natural or manufactured, which, traditionally or for the moment, lends itself to the representation of his intentions.

Childhood play, in experimenting with self-images and images of otherness, is most representative of what psycho-analysis calls the *ego-ideal*—that part of ourselves which we can look up to, at least insofar as we can imagine ourselves as ideal actors in an ideal plot, with the appropriate punishment and exclusion of those who do not make the grade. Thus we experiment with and, in a visionary sense, get ready for a *hierarchy of ideal and evil roles* which, of course, go beyond that which daily life could permit us to engage in. And then, there is always the interplay of the child's imagination with the ritualized fantasy world offered in picture books and in fairy tales, in myths and in parables, which counterpose the best and the worst in human images.

But to attend to epigenesis: in this development the dramatic does not replace, it joins the numinous and the judicial elements, even as it must rely on the elements as yet to be traced ontogenetically: performance and commitment. Nor can any ritual, rite, or ceremony dispense with the dramatic.

The theme of fateful guilt is another dominant theme in all ritual performance, while it comes into its very own in the great tragedies. The play on the toy stage and the plays acted out in drama and ceremonial have certain themes in common which, in fact, induced Freud to give to the dominant inner guilt constellation of the play age the name of a tragic hero: Oedipus. For of all the initiatives dominating the fantasy life of the play age, any thought of actually replacing rather than resembling the parent of the same sex must become taboo, as the price of other more thinkable roles.

What are the forms of psychopathology characterizing

the play age and the neurotic trends emanating from it? It is the weight of excessive guilt that leads to repression in thought and to inhibition in initiative. It is no coincidence that this pathology is suggested in *Hamlet*, the tragedy of the *actor* in every sense of the word. Inhibited in his revenge against his father's murderer and the usurper of his throne and marital bed—and inhibited by the unsettled conflicts of the oedipal stage—he makes a mad spectacle of himself in a *play within a play* and prepares his perdition in and by it. And yet, this perdition is made to seem a salvation from something worse: that pervasive boredom in the midst of "rotten" affluence and power, that malaise and inability to gain pleasure "from either man or woman" which characterizes the inhibition of the dramatic and the denial of the tragic.

In adulthood, the specialized institution for the awe-filled expression of the dramatic is the *stage*. Here, above all, human conflict is projected into a circumscribed space-time in such representative form and supreme condensation that players and audience can experience the catharsis of affects, both timeless and universal. Genuine drama, well played, can shake us to the bones: we know it is "just a play," but because of the dramatic condensation of time and space, we experience something of an intensified reality, unbearably personal and yet miraculously shared.

And yet, the element of dramatic ritualization which enters human life through the very human capacity to play-act also establishes in man a peculiar and pervasive form of ritualism, namely, that of *impersonation*, of role-playing on the stage of reality and history in dead earnestness and, in fact, in matters of mortal danger to the self and others. By this impersonation of a "stance," we do not mean conscious histrionic behavior in the more gifted and amusing sense—that is, the obvious need of human beings to experience themselves as in the center of a stage, or feel off center, out of place, nameless. In infancy, as we saw, the emerging "I" thus feels centered in the converging care of others; this is renewed in childhood play, shared in the identity struggles of youth, and confirmed by one's overall status in later life. The ego-ideal, unlike the forbidding super-ego, provides sanction for selected forms of initiative and idealizes those persons (from parental persons to political figures) who seem to personify ideal usurpations and utopias and who, in turn, have the power to sanction the initiatives of others. But self-idealization as well as the glorification of those called "great" opens the door wide to limitless usurpation: which explains man's compensatory striving for an authenticity always implying a true integration of initiative and guilt, of competence and self-sacrifice. To be denied a true chance of authenticity, however, can force children (and youths) to compulsively assume the role of shameless evildoers—as preferable to being either nameless or overly typed.

SCHOOL AGE AND THE FORMAL: THE METHOD AND THE SCOPE

The *school age* adds another element of ritualization—that of *methodical performance*. Without this, the elements mentioned so far would lack a binding discipline holding them to a minute sequence of competent acts and an over-all quality of craftsmanship and perfection. The mental and emotional eagerness to make material things and facts reveal what can be done with them in order to create new and lasting forms matures only in the school age; or, rather, because it is cognitively ready to arise then, children are sent to schools. There, with varying abruptness, play is transformed into work, game into competition and cooperation, and the freedom of imagination into the duty to perform with full attention to the techniques which make imagination communicable, accountable, and applicable to defined tasks. Ritualization now becomes truly cooperative in the arrangement called school; that is, in the interplay between pupil, teacher, and class. In a prescribed series of tasks structured according to the verbal and the physical nature of the cultural universe, basic techniques are taught which are essential to the participation in the economic and technical system, whether it be predatory and/or agricultural, mercantile and/or industrial, literary and/or scientific. Each of these offers a minute *ritualization of method*, which (this was my point in reporting on first insights into the styles of childhood in a hunting and a fishing tribe) must remain related to a functioning as well as idealized way of life.

We must pause here to consider the style of schooling as a sanction of economic ideals, of forms of competition, and of whatever destruction (of materials, of prey, of competitors, etc.) accompanies constructive work. We saw in our brief example how the Yurok think and speak prayerfully to the salmon to whom they, in fact, promise immortality as a species if only enough specimens will make themselves available for the Yurok's catch and consumption—and, indeed, the yearly dam built across the Klamath River with great ceremony and mirth at the height of the salmon run provides an ample catch for the people, while permitting enough mature salmon to ascend to the spawning territory upriver and, therefore, enough progeny to descend downriver and to disappear into the ocean for a scheduled return. Such performance matched by magic reassurance is also needed by tillers of the soil, for nature must accept being stripped competently of its yearly harvest and yet remain benevolent, and amply so: and by mercantile systems as they amass goods and make commodities out of men, using them, if not as slaves, then as tools and puppets of the market. As industrial civilization expands, we face the very complex question of what happens to the ancient sense of guilt, since human beings also must become machines in order to service machines, must make machines of others, and must turn major decisions over to machines. Everywhere, however, primitive guilt is alleviated by a technical perfection which is adapted to the nature of the segment of the world to be exploited. He who thus contributes to a preordained higher order of perfection *deserves* success, gain, and praise and may—up to a point—forget whom and what he may have exploited or ignored in the process, including his own neglected potentials.

At any rate, the school age introduces the ritualization of that formal aspect of man's performances which is convincing to the senses as it becomes a higher order perceived and yet also participated in. Adding this *formal* aspect to the numinous, judicial, and dramatic elements, we also feel closer to an understanding of the dimensions of any true ritual.

The estrangement of the school age is a sense of *inferiority*, of not being able to live up to the demands of physical performance and mental discipline required for the basic techniques taught. On the other hand, we also perceive the danger of overformalization, perfectionism, and empty ceremonialism; and we must nominate for this stage, too, a ritualistic tendency—here, to pretend that "works" make the man, and technique the truth. Maybe *formalism* will do for this: whatever the name, it must express the fact that human striving for method and logic can also lead to that self-enslavement which makes of each man what Marx called a "craft-idiot," that is, one who for the sake of a proficiency will forget and deny the human context within which it has a significant and maybe dangerous function.

ADOLESCENCE AND THE IDEAL:
THE SELF AND THE TRUTH

The *work role* which we begin to envisage for ourselves at the end of childhood is, under favorable conditions, the most reassuring role of all, just because it confirms us in skills and permits us to recognize ourselves in visible works. But the unrest of puberty and the necessity to leave childhood behind, and the unrest of the times, combine to produce a variety of conflicting self-images, just at the age when we must envisage ourselves not only as worker, but also as mate, parent, and citizen and may feel that we ourselves are being sacrificed to technical perfection and the streamlining of roles. To make brief what I have elaborated on in my other books, the process of identity formation depends on the interplay of what young persons at the end of childhood have come to mean to themselves and what they now appear to mean to those who become significant to them. No wonder that the young are apt to regress in order to stay in touch with the playing child in themselves or "drop out" in order to gain time; or, indeed, grasp at those total ideological visions which combine forceful if vastly simplified and often ruthless answers promising to combine the numinous, the judicial, the dramatic, and the formal—and projecting all self-doubt on "the others."

From here, one could continue in two directions: that is, one could discuss the always surprising and sometimes shocking *spontaneous "rites"* by which adolescents ritualize their relations to each other and demarcate their generation as (slightly or militantly) different both from the adult haves and the infantile have-nots; or one could now turn to *formal rites and rituals*, for it is in the promise of some formal confirmation, induction, or graduation that adolescing human beings are enjoined to become responsible members of their society (or pseudo-species) and often of an elite within it. Only then can they enter the process of becoming an adult in the sense that they can visualize a future in which they will be the everyday ritualizers in their children's lives and, perhaps, occupy ritual positions in the lives of the next generation. Only some *solidarity of conviction* can now tie together all the elements developed in the ontogenetic sequence of ritualizations in a world image provide a coherence of ideas and ideals—unless, indeed, there is a widespread or intensely individual sense of urgent renewal.

The reciprocal mechanisms by which animals complete the interplay of their respective inborn patterns can be said to be paralleled in man only by the whole period of childhood and youth. To be fully grown in the human sense means the readiness to take a place in the technological-political system and also to have certain irreversible values and images intrinsic to one's special kind; which, in turn, means to be ready to exclude (by simple disdain, by moral repudiation, fanatic rebellion, or warfare) inimical identities and outworn or foreign ideologies. I have, therefore, undertaken to delineate the specific crisis which precedes the emergence in youth of a sense of *psychosocial identity* and the readiness for the *ideological style* pervading the ritualizations of the culture. Only an integration of these two processes prepares youth for the alignment of its new strength with the technological and historical trends of the day. And, indeed, where youth (or, at any rate, a decisive part of it) can integrate the ontogenetic elements outlined here in technologically convincing day-by-day activities and can engage in periodical rites and ceremonies of a religious, national, or military nature, its readiness for and almost subservience to the rules of adjustment can offer a picture of astonishing conformity, if often accomplished on the basis of an acceptance of an existing work ethos which may impress outsiders as a pseudo-reality. On the other hand, I have called the estrangement of this stage of life *identity confusion*. This can, of course, be contained in a "way of life" which permits some special leeway in the form of a moratorium devoted to "sprees" or extended periods of experimental and yet prescribed ways of "being different"; while it is often a matter of psychiatric, political, and legal definition whether and where such difference impresses others as borderline psychosis, criminality, dangerous delinquency, or unwholesome fanaticism. Much of youthful "demonstration" can have a bit of all of this as a dramatization (sometimes mocking, sometimes riotous) which serves as a warning that youth's adjustment is not to be taken for granted without the promise of decisive renewal. There are historical identity vacua when the ontogenetic identity crisis is aggravated on a universal scale and met only by an ideological renewal which catches up

with economic and technological changes. This I attempted
to outline in my book on young Luther's personal and universal crisis. The matter can be traced through the revolutionary periods of more recent history, until we see in our
time totalitarian methods of involving new generations
ideologically in staged state rituals combining the numinous
(the Leader's face) and the judicial (loud condemnations
in unison of the "criminals"), the dramatic (parades,
dances, assemblies) and the precise in performance (military precision, mass sports) on a large scale. These attempt
to provide for a whole generation of young individuals an
ideological commitment encompassing perpetual change,
and, in fact, making all traditional (in the sense of pre-
revolutionary) values part of a decidedly *negative identity*.

Nothing, in the end, attests better to the dynamic function of ritualization in everyday life than the very contrast
between the readiness of organized youth to fall in line with
prearranged inductions and confirmations, and the tendency
of de-ritualized youth to improvise counter-ritualizations.
These attempt to guarantee what only a relatively well-
integrated world vision can promise, namely, renewal of
the sense of "I" in solidarity with other "I"'s equally motivated; a management of the infantile conscience by jointly
repudiating some evil otherness or, indeed, by thoughtful
self-abnegation; a shared commitment to ideal images and
a confirmation of the formal methods learned.

In view of all this, it is clear what role *ritualized warfare*
has played throughout history. No doubt, periodical wars
(or the expectation of and preparation for their occurrence) have channeled much ritual need into military
ritualizations with decisive impact on the civilian style of
life. This included the proposition that prospective ene-

mies, up to a point, would grant each other the role of heroes in a joint history.

The ritualistic element reserved for youth I have called *totalism*, that is, a fanatic and exclusive preoccupation with what seems unquestionably ideal within a tight system of ideas. This goes well with the narcissism peculiar to individual youths and the idol-building trend of ideologies; and if it sounds like a partial regression to idolism, this is not without inner logic. The identity stage, furthermore, merges into the stage of *intimacy*—that is, a sustained mutuality in affiliations of work, friendship, and love. This adds an *affiliative* element to the list of ritualizations. Its ritualistic side is a kind of shared narcissim in the form of an *elitism* of exclusive groups. It must be obvious that exactly that demonstrative display of shared tastes and predilections, of enthusiastic opinions and scathing judgments that so often pervade the conversations and actions of young adults bound in love or work, in friendship, or in ideology completes the human form of those instinctive bonds which are confirmed in the greeting ceremonials by which, say, birds signify that they are made for each other —and for an engagement in breeding. In human life it signifies that the respective identities fit (or complement each other) sufficiently to make of two persons a pair, and out of pairs, promising affiliations in productive and procreative life. ~marriage

ADULTHOOD AND RITUAL SANCTION

After *rituals of graduation* from the apprenticeship of youth, *marriage ceremonies* provide for the young adult the "license" to enter those new associations which will transmit a way of life to the coming generation. Religious

rituals are transparent and outspoken in this. But whether
the instituted ceremonies of the adult years call on personal ancestors in the beyond or on culture heroes, on
spirits or gods, on kings, founders, or constitutions, they
first of all are meant to echo and to reaffirm the informal
ritualizations of childhood and youth: for such is the unity
of culture. They thus also sanction the adult; for mature
needs include the need to be reinforced in the role of ritual-
izer, which means not more and not less than to be ready
to become a numinous model in the next generation's eyes
and to act as judge of evil and the transmitter of ideal
values. This adult element in ritualization I would, therefore, call the *generational*. It includes such auxiliary ritualizations as the parental and the didactic, the productive and
the curative, and so on. An adult, as he takes on some authoritative mantle, must be reinforced in the conviction
that "I know what I am doing"—a reassurance often bol-
stered, on the paternal side, by seeing God the Father,
above all the kings, as a parent image (of the same pseudo-
species and, of course, the male sex) who surely knew what
He was doing when He created us in His image; or a
founder, a prophet, or a great mind who convincingly an-
nounced the principles of a new world image. Now that
women have made us face it, and at a time when patriarchal
authority as such has suffered much exposure, it is becoming irreversibly clear how much male dominance has relied on ritualized authority. In view of the oppressive re-
sponsibilities implied in all authority, it is no wonder that
the specific form of ritualism corresponding to the generational ritualization is that of a self-convinced and yet
spurious usurpation of authority—*authoritism* if you will.
But here we come to the adults' part in the ritualizations

already described and to real rituals, a topic to be touched upon, but not to be treated here.

A word, however, about the "old man's reasons," which play such a role in ritual life. Its burden of ritualization is, I would think, the *integral*, which affirms the meaning of the cycle of life. As I read Blake, he is suggesting that old reasons are, at their best, blessed (again) by playful childlikeness. The traditional role of the old as the personification of ritual wisdom would speak for this interpretation. Yet modern ways of living and maybe the experience of seeing many, rather than just a few tough and exceptional persons, reach old age could make one wonder whether Blake may not have meant to imply that old reasons even as toys can be a bit childish. For the pre-senile years, with all their unavoidable *despair* and *disgust*, I have postulated the strength of a simple *integrity* which is directly perceived by children; wherefore old people and children feel an affinity for each other. But, of course, old age also has its own ritualism, namely, the unwise pretense of being wise: *sapientism*, then?

We can see now what rituals must accomplish: by combining and renewing the ritualizations of childhood and affirming generative sanction, they help to consolidate adult life once its commitments and investments have led to the creation of new persons and to the production of new things and ideas. And, of course, by tying life cycle and institutions into a meaningful whole, they create a sense of immortality not only for the leaders and the elite but also for every participant. And there can be little doubt that the ritualization of everyday life permits, and even demands, that adults forget death as the inscrutable background of all life, and give priority to the absolute reality of world views shared with others of the same geography, history, and technology. By means of ritual, in fact, death becomes the meaningful boundary of such reality.

I have now listed some elements I can discern in the ontogeny of ritualization, and I will offer their approximate epigenesis in a table intended to help in discussion and research. It shows how each of the ritualizations which helped to integrate the stages of ontogeny provide a basic element for the major rituals which help to hold some basic institutions of society together, namely, faith in a cosmic order, a sense of law and justice, a hierarchy of ideal and evil roles, the fundamentals of technology, and ideological perspectives.

As to the whole process, it should be noted that there can be no prescription for either ritualization or ritual, for, far from being merely repetitive or familiar in the sense of habituation, any true ritualization, while ontogenetically grounded, is yet pervaded with the spontaneity of surprise: it is an unexpected renewal of a recognizable order in potential chaos. Ritualization thus depends on that blending of surprise and recognition which is the soul of creative interplay, reborn out of instinctual chaos, confusion of identity, and social anomie.

ONTOGENY OF RITUALIZATION

	NUMINOUS	JUDICIOUS	DRAMATIC	FORMAL	IDEOLOGICAL	GENERATIONAL SANCTION
infancy	mutuality of recognition					
early childhood		discrimination of good and bad				
play age			dramatic elaboration			
school age				rules of performance		
adolescence					solidarity of conviction	
elements in adult rituals						

Re-Ritualization

BUT NOW, past the midpoint of this book, do I hear some among my readers protest a certain nostalgic conservatism in my acknowledgment of the power of ritualization and ritual? Do I really think they have ever "worked" and are indispensable to personality and society? And even if such a "natural" scheme is discernible in the social animals, and in primitive and even in some traditional societies, the very core of what I am charting here seems now in hopeless jeopardy, and maybe lacks relevance in an overpopulated and polluted, manufactured and mechanized world. Granted the evolutionary significance of ritualization in man, will I be able to shirk the question of how fading rituals are now giving way to fabricated ritualizations of a new kind, dictated above all by methods of mass communication and maybe not recognizable to the ethologist's or the psychoanalyst's overtrained eye? As I said myself, new sources of numinous and judicial affirmation as well as of dramatic and aesthetic representations can obviously come only from a new spirit embodying an eventual identification of the whole human species with itself; for are we not all, in a phrase now so fashionable and yet so often deeply meant, "human beings"?

As to another epigenetic chart, have my students not long suspected that all these neat listings are my own cere-monial reassurances? Could it be that only the privileged can afford a life cycle? Maybe my charts, these skeptics say, are a reasonably approximate guide to the study of life, but they can also be used to deny what is obvious, namely, that many adults are defined by the very fact that the playfulness of the stages has gone out of them—and not only the poor, deprived of all leeway, but also the fortunate ones who were given so much leeway it has paralyzed them and so much affluence it has stifled them. And as for the leeway they gave to their children, what, at the end, did it do for many but take the game out of growing up and eventually help to ruin even sincere rebellion?

To all of these reservations, let me say here only this: To explore the various ways in which today's technological civilization attempts, with more universal and more hazard-ous improvisations than any before, to re-ritualize man's early years as well as the relations of adults to one another—will, indeed, call for much interdisciplinary discussion.[6] But I would point out that in the sporadic revolt of youth in the 1960s the whole grave question of universal re-ritualization came, indeed, to expression. That revolt, like the whole counterculture, expressed a deep malaise over the loss of imagination and the costly denial of that loss on the part of leaders who continued to rely on the young to "serve" in a bloody cause which they themselves felt impotent to end. It was, as our introductory quotations showed, the fake reality of a colonial war which relied all the more on technological means of overkill as it became more desperately unsure of itself. This, to some of the young, suddenly seemed unbearable as a "way of life" to live in—and to die (and kill) for.

But as to the question of the nature of re-ritualization, I can only reassert here what alone is and can be the psychoanalyst's job, namely, to help trace the way in which the past, ontogenetic or phylogenetic, in life history or in history, is built into the present: for such insight is needed to help free the present for its future tasks. And it is here that the ethologist and the psychoanalyst have corresponding jobs: the one clarifies the power of what was once called the instinctive pattern, the other that of the so-called instinctual forces and the structure of the individual and the communal mind. And even as an evolutionary forecast might have to take into account the immensely slow velocity of evolutionary change as against rapidly changing historical and technological perspectives, a psychoanalytic forecast would have to keep in mind, in particular, the slow rate of changeability in some of man's archaic inner propensities and, among them, the need for a world image linking everyday life with some universal vision.[7]

Now, old-fashioned ritualizations may be easily abandoned in the emergence of a new cosmos held together by the scientific and technological ethos, by the methods of mass communication, or by the replacement of "ordained" authorities with an indefinite sequence of experts correcting and complementing each other. But as modern technology rightfully attaches its own ritualizations to necessities and opportunities in homes and at work, and as world-wide communication creates new and more universal parliaments, new prophets will rush in to occupy places left vacant by vanishing ritualization. It remains our job, then, to continue to chart the slow laws of ontogeny which man, when he becomes too carelessly utopian, neglects only at great danger. For with each child born, new and yet very old potentials arise which make specific demands on new world views—a fact we must keep in mind as we turn to what we can discern of the function and the fate of *shared* visions.

In conclusion, however, I must confess to the belief that in our day signs of a re-ritualization of everyday life abound amid some disintegration of traditional forms and that they can be recognized by their simple vitality—and playfulness.

III

Shared Visions

Visions on the Wall

I BEGAN THIS BOOK with one child's play construction, reviewed some play theories, and came to the conclusion that I have no reason to revise the suggestion made in my first book, namely, that *play* on a toy stage is only one model of the human proclivity to project onto a circumscribed "microsphere" an arrangement of figures which dramatizes a moment of fate. In child's play we saw the model for the creative vision which later uses a circumscribed field, a "plane" (and to ex-plain means to spread something out for clearer comprehension), a stage, or a blueprint to gain mastery over what he is in the process of becoming by means of evolutionary and historical, technical and personal developments. But I also had to point to the fear, the anxiety, and the dread which overwhelm man, small or big, when he finds his hoped-for leeway checkmated by inner inhibitions or by blind circumstances, a fate imposed on him by visible or invisible enemies: in fact, I indicated that where man does not have enemies he often must invent them in order to create boundaries against which he can assert the leeway of the new man he must become.

The ontogenetic cultivation of a viewpoint, I then explained in the second part, is accomplished by a minute *ritualization* of daily life, which leads from the smallest items of personal interplay to the ceremonial get-togethers of cultural events—all saying, "This is the way *we* see, and say, and do things, and it is the *human* way." Visions are grounded in facts verifiable in some detail and yet arranged to fit within a cosmology and an ideology that unite groups of human beings in mutual actualizations.

I will now describe the manifestation of such visions in a number of fields, beginning with those closest to me by avocation and vocation, namely, art and psychoanalysis. This, at any rate, permits me to begin again by sharing a visual experience. Recently, Hellmut Wohl gave a paper in San Francisco, "On Point of View." [1] In this, he related the formal perspective of Renaissance painting to the Christian faith it was to propagate, and both perspective and faith to the need for a vision of hope.

Aesthetic vision offers a model for the formulation of ideas in terms of a coherent point of view. [It thus] signifies the reaffirmation of basic trust—perhaps the deepest criterion for the measure of coherence that a point of view represents. Finally, aesthetic vision provides both an ideal and a standard of that wholeness which a point of view imparts to reality.

In the De Young Museum, we saw the Van Borsig *Annunciation* ascribed to a Flemish master of the early sixteenth century. In all its anonymity and simplicity it

immediately seemed to us to unite many of the basic elements of man's playful vision, from its ontogenetic origins
in what can be seen to its most existential visionary meaning. An *Annunciation*, of course, is a visitation announc-
ing the Eternal Prospect, the expectation that the child to
be born will be the Child who will forever save in man
some portion of what childhood promises: The "King-
dom." There is Mary, then, the to-be-elect. Becoming
aware of the angel's presence and glance, she lowers an
open book, and we can see that the page she had studied
(and a page, too, is a framed visual field) is "illuminated":
it shows the biblical theme of a kneeling figure before an
apparition of light—is it Moses, the prophet of the old law,
as Christ will be of the new? But Mary is almost over-
shadowed by the presence of the angelic messenger with
the commanding glance, who brings the word that within
her will be the Child, the guarantor of a New Man. And,
indeed, the Holy Spirit, the agent, can be seen floating
down on a golden and piercing ray of light.

The stage, in the foreground of which all this takes
place, has two doorframes opening up on two rooms in the
background. The one behind Mary reveals her bed; the
other leads our eyes straight to two further frames: a window opening on the town; and, beside it, an open triptych
with rounded panels: in its brightness, it could easily be
mistaken for another window (a "wind-eye"). It, too,
shows a kneeling figure before an apparition of light, and
we are reminded that to face the east means to be "oriented"
in a world in which the darkness of night always opens
up on the dawn.

If I pointed out that the play constructions of children
as well as corresponding visions seem to reveal a need of

human consciousness to be central to the world rather than shunted to the periphery and to be chosen in one's newness rather than negligible, then we must certainly recognize Mary's womb as being, at that moment, in the center of the universe—as is, indeed, that of any woman pregnant with child, and every child newly born: new eyes to be set on the world, a new face to be recognized, a new name becoming the mark of a new "I," and (who knows) a new person full of a grace not yet betrayed by the "human condition."

Yet, to encompass the total world view of which this small picture portrays only the promising beginning, and to envisage all the dimensions we recognized in our "ordinary" play construction, we would have to include such other paintings as those that might surround an *Annunciation* on the walls of any studio, any church, or any museum. One picture may depict that child as the grown Son of Man, his hand raised, in the persuasive gesture of blessing; another crying his last cry, his hands nailed to a cross, in the dreadful night of Golgotha. One may show the Son of God benevolently saluting the saved and elect in Heaven, another majestically discarding those to be damned in Hell, another depict one of the crowned heads who with ceremonial splendor have represented the crucified carpenter's son through history; in another, we may see spread before us a battlefield, hallowed *"in hoc signo,"* with the felled infidels piled up in wounded and dying agony.

Thus, only a whole ensemble of themes, linking a special creation in the past with the certainty of a prophesied future, provides the Eternal Prospect with a perspective that gives meaning to all births and deaths and the enigmas in between. And once established, a new world view acquires not only a renewed identity symbolical of eternal renewal, but also techniques and rituals, hierarchies and battle lines, which vastly elaborate the original vision of the believing "I" bound with other mortal "I"s through one divine "I"— the one that assuredly Is. Only thus does man feel protected against the doom of some primal curse—is it that of non-existence?—and able to face the verdict of a last judgment where only the elect few will be saved, while all others— those excluded from choices—will perish. Thus we make a political deal with mortality and infinity; and let us not overlook the fact that the most transcendent of visions will become rooted in establishments (such as churches) that politicize existential needs and come to live off human alone-ness and death; for whether or not we can truly perceive ourselves as physically dead, our soul fears above all to be alone and to be inactivated in eternity. (For the dread of a forfeited identity, I found a supreme formula on the tomb-stone of one who was beheaded in the very century when this *Annunciation* was painted: "My youth is gone, and yet I am but young; I saw the world, and yet I was not seen.")

That quiet *Annunciation*, then, in which the light and spirit, the face and the word come together, derives its persuasiveness from the recurrent cataclysmic dread of total darkness and spiritual death, of facelessness and meaning-lessness. But let us not forget that to be magically convinc-ing, the painter must be in technical command of an art providing a living style for the play with forms. Only then will his work appeal to the deepest needs of the viewer and confirm faith with demonstrated truth.

To keep this in mind is of the essence, as we mention other "frames" or spheres—some seemingly totally foreign

to each other. That a framed picture may share some configurations with a dream or with the proscenium of a theater
is not difficult to claim; but that theater and theory may
have common roots in experience as well as in language
may be more so. And yet, these two words have in common
"visible or visualized spheres arousing fascination and belief." In the same way, many words which we use every
day have emerged from word roots related to seeing: that
a fact is evident because any willing person can see it—
that is evident. Yet, there are very central words which
contain a linguistic root marking them as visible: an idea as
a model in the inner eye; history as a visualized continuum
of events; and wisdom as a final overview—with some wit
to spare. Thus does all true perspective affirm the original
organ of comprehension in an imaginative creature born
with stereoscopic vision—and a need for a perspective and
an outlook.

Perspective at its best gives a transcendent order to what
is visible from a given position in space, and leads from what
is closest to a point revealed in the far distance. It thus opens
and limits us to our point of view, foreshortening all that
is distant and hiding all that happens to be behind the objects seen. Far from deserving to be taken for granted,
however, an elaborate emphasis on perspective is itself an
expression of a particular world view. By the same token,
in gloriously affirming a visible world order as well as the
orderliness of vision, art can give an aesthetic glow even to
subjects of damnation and despair. It can illuminate the
grandest illusions and outshine with realism itself the very
lowness of daily life. We treasure Rembrandt for illuminating so grandly and so simply the transcendence of everyday
hereness.

The Dream Screen

As I NOW TURN to my own field of observation, psychoanalysis, it seems only one step (and it was so in my own life) from the pictures on the wall to the images dreamed at night.

The late Bertram Lewin has provided us with a term which can help us to find in psychoanalytic introspection a counterpart to those toy tables and playing boards and game fields which we have been discussing. He called the background on which we see our dreams the dream screen. In his book, *The Image and the Past*, he is fully aware of the role of vision in the dreams and the memories which patients report and which psychoanalysts hear, meditate upon, and interpret. In discussing the question of what goes on in the psychoanalyst's head as he listens to his patient, Lewin suspects (with others) that the psychoanalyst's remarkable ability to listen to many people for hours must to some extent rely on a "sublimated scopophilia," that is, a higher kind of voyeurism which permits him to endure long working days visualizing what he hears.[2] But so must the patient translate into words what often "comes to mind" as images on an inner screen—and Freud said, long ago: "Even in those whose memory is not normally of a visual type, the earliest recollections of childhood retain far into life the quality of sensory vividness."

But if vision is, as we saw, the basic organizer of the sensory universe and if the beholding of one person's face by another is the foundation of a sense of mutuality, then the classical psychoanalytic treatment situation itself is an exquisite deprivation experiment. Freud created the arrangement, it is said, because he did not like to be stared at, which can only mean that a patient's avid wish to see the therapist's facial response interfered with the theory builder's wish to think before he responded. But it is also the genius of this clinical invention that it systematically provokes the patient's "free" verbal associations by creating a visual void, which invites the rushing in of old images seeking a healing mutuality. Above all, this setting serves to intensify what we call transference, that is, a transfer to the unseen listener of important personages of the past, and especially the primal parent—and this often with all the dread of being abandoned and the rage over being ignored. All this, of course, is eminently instructive in regard to what "down there" is left over from "way back" and can be deeply and uniquely therapeutic. But we also know that classical psychoanalysis is a cure for which a patient must be relatively healthy in the first place and gifted for this specific ascetic combination of introspection and verbali-

zation. And as, sooner or later, every field must become
aware of the way in which its principal procedure in-
fluences the nature of the observed, we will, in our context,
pursue some of the fate of the visual in the classical procedure.

Let me tell, then, of the shortest dream ever reported to
me. I have come back to it over the years because it demon-
strates how a clinical datum of utmost brevity can prove to
be like the hub of a wheel in which a great number of
meanings are conjoined. It was the first dream reported
by a young woman patient. German-speaking, but versed
in Romance languages, the young woman reported, in a
tone half shy and half daring me to see what I could make
of *that*, a dream consisting only of the word S[E]INE—
lit up against a dark background. The first letter E was in
brackets. The whole word obviously referred to the river
that flows through Paris: and, indeed, it had been in Paris
and on leaving the Louvre that the patient as a young girl
had first been overcome by the symptom of agoraphobia
that now brought her to analysis. But if she had seen a
disturbing picture there, she did not remember it. And,
indeed, the form of her dream suggested that what she
saw so overly clearly in neon-light letters corresponded
to some dark spot in her mind: maybe some amnesia. But
what did those letters say? There seemed to be a linguistic
puzzle hidden in this one word. "To see," in German, is
sehen, a word that is often pronounced like the French
"Seine." So, we have "seen by the Seine." But *seine* is also
a German word, meaning "his"; and if we cross out the
letter in brackets, we have the Latin word *sine*, meaning
"without." Taken together, the word puzzle seems to say
that the patient, by the Seine, had seen (somebody) with-

out his (something). In the course of her free associations, and along some detours, the patient eventually remembered a picture that had shocked her deeply: it was a *Circumcision of Christ*. Being Catholic, she had, as a curious small girl, guiltily wondered what was behind the Savior's loincloth: here the Christ child was without it and defenselessly exposed to ritual surgery. Her shock, however, had been, as we say, overdetermined: for the picture, it soon became plausible, had reminded her of a most traumatic experience in childhood when she had been catheterized by her father, a pediatrician, because of a bladder condition that was reducing the flow of urine. This memory caused in the patient a deep panic, and increased a certain squirming on the couch which now appeared to represent the apprehension that something like that medical procedure was going to be repeated in the psychoanalytic situation. She was, however, able to describe the early experience in emotional detail: besides the pain endured, the shame and a certain rage over having to expose herself to her father had been intense, for while she herself could not see what he saw and did, the procedure did make her void. Those versed in these matters will note that in psychoanalytic libido theory we include the age of five, when all this happened, in the phallic (or, as I prefer to call it, the infantile genital and locomotor) stage, and it will be obvious how traumatic at that stage an event was that both immobilized and exposed the little girl—in an "oedipal" context.

This dream eventually proved strategic in helping to clarify the patient's early neurosis and personality development. But if we now ask in what way this first dream also dwelt on the "psychoanalytic situation," we must turn to the "initiation" of the procedure. When she had come for her first hour, I had informed her that she was to lie on the couch, facing away from me; and she was to let her thoughts come freely and to verbalize them candidly, no matter how painful or shameful they might seem to her. Now, in presenting me with the dream, she seemed to challenge me even as she declared herself ready to play my game. The basic theme of the dream obviously compared the Christ child's and her own predicament to the clinical ritual commanding her to assume a supine position in which she could not see me but was to permit what in my trade we, indeed, refer to as the "free flow" of verbal associations so that I might detect unconscious ideas that might prove embarrassing to her. The idea of flow, at any rate, connects the image of the river with the urinary focus of her memories and the basic requirement of her treatment.

The special combination of rage and shame aroused by this all too suggestive situation finally leads us to the meaning of the bracketed letter E. This being my initial, it suggested some trick of "transference," that is, a transfer on the psychoanalyst of highly conflicted feelings originally attached to a significant figure in childhood. In this sense, it can be seen to reveal the further thought that she might wish to "turn the tables" and to expose *me:* a mocking projection of both the Savior's and her own predicament. Here, then, the patient's passively suffered self-exhibition, according to a well-known reversal, is actively turned against me with an aggressive voyeurism which, in fact, is also natural for the very stage of childhood when she was traumatized. This interpretation could only confound the patient's embarrassment, but also led to some (luckily not

infrequent) shared laughter over the tricks of the unconscious which can condense—and give away—all these meanings in one word.

But here I have followed only one main trend of thought
suggested in the patient's multilingual dream puzzle. The
French-speaking reader will have missed, at least by association, some reference to the word *sein*—breast. And, indeed, the patient eventually remembered another painting
that had shocked her. Ascribing it to Rubens, she recalled
a goddess with six breasts—an obvious countervision to the
Circumcision, for it added a theme of utmost plenitude
where the other theme so sharply subtracted. Yet, this was
too fleshly an affirmation of femininity for the young girl,
who at the time had felt attracted to as well as disquieted
by the sensual emphasis in women's dress (décolleté) and
the seductive masculine mores of Parisian life. While the
first picture, then, pointed to an infantile trauma suffered
during a specific infantile stage, the second symbolized the
cultural atmosphere which in the adolescent girl had
aroused voyeuristic and exhibitionistic wishes and thus set
the libidinal tone for the whole traumatic and, as it were,
re-repressive experience, now relived in the psychoanalytic
situation.

We can, then, see in this first dream of an admittedly
rather "classical" case an infantile and an adolescent
trauma in interplay with the psychoanalytic situation. A
parallelism of such clarity that is revealed so promptly is,
of course, rare. It must usually be reconstructed from many
obscure details over a long period of treatment. But the
example may make it plausible that in thus enforcing the
patient's concentration on the sequence of emerging images,

the treatment intensified a "natural" self-healing process, which Bertram Lewin formulated thus:

All recapturing of the pictorial past, whether as dream picture, screen memory, new memory of repressed traces, etc., could include, besides the more obvious wish fulfillments and defensive formations, an equivalent of an attempt at explanation and cure.[3]

Freud had gone further in claiming that even

The delusions of patients appear to me to be the equivalents of the constructions which we build up in the course of an analytic treatment—attempts at explanation and cure.[4]

Finally, it must interest us that this dream leads to two "visions on the wall" and especially to one that belongs in the same religious context as does our *Annunciation:* somewhere they could very well hang in the same hall. And in both of them we can see at work the particular proclivity of the ego which interests us here, namely a private space-time orientation in interplay with a world view which gives structure and meaning to the multiplicity of experience. It must be clear that the patient's traumatic reaction to the extreme imagery of the *Circumcision* was codetermined by her ready identification with the Christ child in his infantile predicament and, in fact, in the whole vision of suffering suggested by Christ's life and death. Her neurosis was codetermined by the fact that this identification had been elaborated into a deeply masochistic vision, with many irrational aspects. In her late adolescence, this vision was in intense conflict with another one which came into full bloom in the Parisian atmosphere: the exhibitionistic and voyeuristic indulgence in erotic temptation. These coexisting visions aggravated her confusion by alternately suggesting two totally different identities: her agoraphobia resolved this conflict by making her a patient. But the promise of a psychoanalytic cure opened up a third vision, namely, the promise of enlightenment, as a mediator between sexuality and spirituality. Finally, the humor and the artistry of this play on the dream screen certified not only to the tricky powers of the unconscious but also to the dreamer's specific linguistic giftedness and expressed the hope that the new woman, liberated by psychoanalysis from her infantile bondage, would see the light, would be able to move and look around freely and use her talents. Thus, to the ancient Christian and the modern French visions was added the Freudian version of Enlightenment.

Our example shows that even dreams can be shared visions, or *inter*play. We know, at any rate, another's dream only as it has been communicated, although we then often feel as if we had seen it. But we will never know, except for our own dreams, what the difference is between an incommunicable dream and one we are eager or are expected to tell. Once we set out to study our own dreams, furthermore, we may well dream them in order to study them, and that means in order to prove some anticipations and to communicate these—as Freud did so grandiosely. Patients, in turn, know that they will or should report their dreams, and this in the context of a therapeutic style: wherefore Jungian and Freudian patients, for example, seem to differ radically in their manifest dream imagery. Their dreams, in fact, can be seen to reflect the vision of the respective "schools"—a therapeutic communality, then, maybe seasoned with a bit of obliging "politics"? All such relativity, however, once understood, only confirms that dreams do not lie.

Our example, then, illustrates forcefully what we may yet have to work out in much less obvious contexts, namely, what the "classical" psychoanalytic setting habitually maximizes: verbal freedom connoting a new leeway for consciousness, the awareness of unconscious themes, and the recovery of the past. But we can also see what is put aside with the erect position: above all, facial confrontation and locomotion, and some leeway of ad-gressiveness in a live situation of mutual give-and-take. And if, indeed, any laboratory of observation must be studied in its characteristic "equations" and its influence on the kinds of data observed and the kinds of concepts arrived at, then we have to conclude in this context that the setting minimizes "political" behavior almost systematically and thus (as Alfred Adler long ago protested) those aspects of humanity which Marx, in a grandiose division of labor by historical polarization, during the same century elaborated into a materialistic world image.

I have already wondered aloud in a number of contexts what the consequence of this overweening fact may have had for psychoanalytic conceptualization. Psychoanalytic attention, obviously, concentrates on inner events and, indeed, attempts to comprehend the interplay of what are referred to as "inner agencies" and even "inner institutions": the ego, for example, in relation to the super-ego. Social institutions, in turn, are referred to as part of the "outer world"—almost a gigantic outer screen on which inner events are projected. I will, in a moment, say more about the way in which the inner and the outer institutions are, in fact, complementary and exist with and by each other. In the meantime, what happened on one patient's inner screen may at least suggest that case histories could teach us more about the fact that individuals live, often more than they know and profess, by collective visions, whether in the form of religious world images or of political ones, whether these visions seem overly conscious as wordy ideologies or shining new deals or are only vaguely conscious as a "way of life"; whether they have become a deeply held genuine belief system or remain a more or less artful web of inner and outer deals.

Such studies might help us to understand better that any revolutionary method of treatment worthy of its name offers itself as a new world vision. A discussion of the world image implicit in psychoanalytic practice and theory could well begin with Roy Schafer's impressive reflections on "The Psychoanalytic Vision of Reality," in which he ascribes to the psychoanalytic vision the stances of the dramatic: the tragic and comic, the ironic and romantic. He, too, speaks of "visions of reality" and says:

The term vision implies judgments partly rooted in subjectivity, that is, in acts of imagination and articles of faith, which, however illuminating and complex they may be, necessarily involve looking at reality from certain angles and not others. As visions influence the determination of facts and their interrelations and implications, clashes between visions cannot be settled by simple appeals to "the evidence." It would not be correct to regard these clashes merely as matters of opinion.[5]

In pursuing his own vision of the psychoanalytic "vision of reality," he professes to an image of the psychoanalyzed new man which is undoubtedly close to Freud's therapeutic and philosophical mood:

As issues of responsibility and choice enter into an analysis, additional emphasis falls on tragic comprehension. Then the analysed patient may even knowingly and regretfully—but rightly—make choices that he knows will involve him in suffering, while at the same time he will also be much freer to foster the possibilities for pleasure in his life and reduce the objective danger and pain he encounters.[6]

But it must be admitted again that this strong dramatic element in psychoanalysis, in all its affinity to literary culture, had to share also the scientific vision of its day, as is so obvious in its quasi-anatomical and physicalistic terms. And it will be important to study how such a "tragic" vision, through its career in the modern world, not only adjusted to the political vision of the self-made man, but also seemed to suggest mechanistic stances that were eagerly absorbed as a pseudo-vision of the "fully analyzed" human being who would be master of his drives and fantasies, socially adjusted, and facing reality itself. How this came about will have to be studied in a historical self-appraisal—for which, we must emphasize in conclusion, no other field seems to be better equipped.

In such an undertaking, it may help to have the sanction of another creator of new paradigms, who—it turns out—can tell us much about the role of play and of vision even in the exactest of sciences.

Einstein's Puzzles

GERALD HOLTON, in his recent work, makes us understand the importance of visualization in the work of that prime theory builder, Albert Einstein. It must interest us that as a child Einstein was an avid block builder and fitter of jig-saw-puzzle pieces; but he was not interested in learning to speak when most children do. Holton reports, "It is well known that, as a child of four or five, Einstein experienced what he called 'a wonder' when his father showed him a simple magnetic compass. It was an experience to which Einstein often referred." [7] Truly a toy for him!

Holton rightly makes much of the fact that young Einstein in the *Gymnasium*—a kind of classical high school—failed foreign languages even as in 1895 he failed the entrance examination to the Polytechnic Institute in Zurich and had to go back to school. Only then he found a school which almost a century before had been founded by and (so Holton surmises) was still a cultural heir to the vision of the great Pestalozzi, whose main principle had been that *Anschauung*, a personal and yet systematic way of *looking* at things, was the absolute foundation of all learning. And "everything somehow changed for Einstein," from an encouragement of his way of thinking that eventually led to relativity, to a new appreciation of friendship. Holton concludes:

The objects of imagination were to Einstein evidently persuasively real, visual materials which he voluntarily and playfully could reproduce and combine, analogous, perhaps, to the play with shapes in a jigsaw puzzle. The key words are *Bild* (image) and *Spiel* (play); and once alerted to them, one finds them with surprising frequency in Einstein's writings.[8]

Toward the end of his life, Einstein mused "that he was brought to the formulation of relativity theory in good part because he kept asking himself questions concerning space and time that only children wonder about." And he specified in 1945:

Taken from a psychological viewpoint, [a certain] combinatory play seems to be the essential feature in productive thought—before there is any connection with logical construction in words or other kinds of signs which can be communicated to others. The above mentioned elements are, in my case, of visual and some of muscular type. Conventional words or other signs have to be sought for laboriously only in a secondary stage, when the mentioned "*associative play*" is sufficiently established and can be reproduced at will.[9]

To this, he added in his autobiographical notes (written at the age of sixty-seven):

With what right—the reader will ask—does this man operate so carelessly and primitively with ideas in such a problematic realm without making even the least effort to prove anything? My defense: All our thinking is of this nature of a free play with concepts [*Begriffen*]: the justification for this play lies in the measure of survey over the experience of the senses which we are able to achieve with its aid.[10]

The word translated here as "survey" is *Uebersicht*, "overview," with the connotation of a free scanning of a wide horizon, which brings us back to the matter of *Anschauung:* a way of looking at things that is both focused and encompassing.

How much all this is a highly personal version of a universal aspect of genius only comparative studies could show; but I do feel that it throws much light on the "cosmological" aspect of scientific thought. What is called cosmological, however, again has its origin in the German word *Weltanschauung*, the core of which, namely, *schauen*, is hard to translate satisfactorily, since it combines an inner "way of looking" at things with an intent viewing of phenomena. Maybe the somewhat too precious "to behold" would come closest. To get from here to what in these pages we call a world view, we must quote Einstein once more:

Man seeks to form for himself, in whatever manner is suitable for him, a simplified and lucid image of the world [*Bild der Welt*], and so to overcome the world of experience by striving to replace it to some extent by this image. This is what the painter does, and the poet, the speculative philosopher, the natural scientist, each in his own way. Into this image and its formation he places the center of gravity of his emotional life, in order to attain the peace and serenity that he cannot find within the narrow confines of swirling, personal experience.[11]

Note Einstein's way of combining in the one word "swirling" all that our central, active, selective, aware,

effective, and inclusive ego fears most. In relating this to
the power of new world views, Einstein cautions:

The theoretical physicists' picture of the world [Weltbild] is one
among all the possible pictures. It demands vigorous precision in all
the description of relationships. Therefore the physicist must content himself from the point of view of subject matter with "por-
traying the simplest occurrences which can be made accessible to
our experience"; all more complex occurrences cannot be reconstructed without the necessary degree of subtle accuracy and logical perfection. "Supreme purity, clarity, and certainty, at the cost
of completeness." [12]

At the end, Holton points to Einstein's unusual flair for
playing with *polarities:* space and time, energy and mass,
inertia and gravitation, wave and particle. He first called his
theory the *Invarianten Theory*, although it was to become
famous—and, for a while, infamous—as the more sensational
theory of relativity.

Thus Einstein and the cultural and even political history
of relativity could interest us from another angle. If relativity as a theory is in the center of a new way of viewing
the universe, its craftsmanship can be admiringly affirmed
only by the few who understand both theory and method,
while it becomes a vague world view to the many who
have no choice but to believe the experts even if its connotations seem quite disconcerting as they seem to upset
some firm perspectives of the previously accepted view of
the world. We should not laugh off the fact that official
National Socialist Germany called relativity a Jewish vision
and denounced Einstein's mind as diabolic: for there were,
as well, non-party-line scientists in Germany who considered Einstein's views a countervision to all that was
"classical" and, therefore, not only improbable in fact but
immoral in intent—"abominable" (*abscheulich*). Neither is

it enough to explain the subsequent semi-divine status of Einstein's countenance in the world (his eyes, indeed, full of *Anschauung*) as a mere result of the fact that his theory eventually was proven. In fact, I would suggest that even today, and especially in the social sciences, pervasive resistances exist to thinking in terms of relativity. If Freud likened the trauma he himself had caused to mankind by questioning the sovereignty of consciousness to the trauma of Copernicus' dethroning of the earth from its central place in the physical universe, and Darwin's disproof of man's separate and elect status in the world of creatures, he could well have included Einstein among those who upset mankind's peace of mind.

A word about Copernicus—and "swirling." Following Freud, we have tended to view his heliocentric world view as an ascetic admission, due to inescapable scientific evidence, that mankind's earth was not the centerpiece even of the most immediate world space. This interpretation seems to point to the essential ego need for some central position in a world view. Yet Copernicus enveloped his new theory in an aesthetic vision which gave to this abandoned earth at least a "pleasing" place in a new and by no means ascetic imagery of the world. In his *De revolutionibus orbium coelestium*, he assigned to the sun "a throne in the middle of all things," from where "it could throw light on everything at once." In line with thinkers of antiquity, he thus ascribed to the sun the nature of a divine body that not only was visible but also could "see all," and, therefore, had the capacity of thought as well as the power to navigate the universe. And he developed the vision (in psychoanalysis, we might call it a grandiose "primal scene") of an elemental interplay between the earth, the sun, and the moon by which the earth, once a year, was impregnated with new life. Churchmen, of course, did not appreciate the cosmological license Copernicus took. Luther, for example, thundered against it as counter-scriptural: Did not Joshua command the sun to stand still; and did not this prove that it was, in fact, moving? But Copernicus' vision reminds us of Einstein's claim that the great scientist's basic state of feeling is "akin to that of the worshipper or of one who is in love." In the meantime, it remains, of course, essential that Copernicus' central thesis only expanded prophetically and endowed with the vision of a new reality a factual cosmic circumstance that was emerging from direct astronomical evidence. But in doing this, he claimed for the new world order those elements of numinosity, of seeing and being seen, which we have postulated as basic for a sense of hope, and he did so in the time of mankind's greatest danger of feeling, indeed, "swirled" about in the universe.

Here is the place to remind ourselves of the stake in all visions, not only for the experts who own them and, therefore, must own up to them in controversy, but also for every individual living in a given period when a variety of religious, scientific, and ideological views vie with each other. The nature of the human ego, an evolutionary fact as decisive and as paradoxical as any, has a vital stake in all theories which attest to man's centeredness in the universe. But in its search for mastery, it also supports the infinite inquisitiveness of science which is then apt to make that centeredness relative, whether it allocates to the earth a different corner in the universe or makes man's proud will dependent on unconscious motivation. Humanity, therefore, forever struggles for a centered quality of existence by reconciling the incomparably greater awareness and the greater power which science provides with the fact that it also makes man lonelier in the universe and more responsible for himself. This, no doubt, has facilitated the historical paradox of modern man's readiness, under certain conditions, to embrace totalistic revolutionary ideologies which insist on minute re-ritualizations in daily life; while countries whose world view includes a revolutionary rebirth in the past undergo repetitive crises of conflicting ritualizations as they adapt their national dreams to modern dimensions.

A National Dream

As we proceed from scientific to political world visions, it is obvious that the average individual, who is neither a vision builder nor swayed by delusional omnipotence, can boast of a sense of centrality in the world and leeway in action only as he participates in a world image of proven actuality—in the interplay of work activities, intimate affiliations, and political doings of a community and its leaders. A good leader, in turn, is an individual who can instill qualities of an active existence and inspire in his followers a sense of being chosen by their very choice of him.

But what would be the best word for a "shared vision" operative in the inner world of individual motivation as well as in political arenas, big and small? Maybe "world view" will have to do; and my doubt may be nothing but a remnant of my humanist schooling in Germany where there was only one word for it, as familiar to every student as it was to young Einstein: *Weltanschauung*. By then, however, that word had itself become a kind of ritualistic centerpiece of the German *Kultur,* and, in those imperialistic days, had assumed a rather strenuous stance which in national defeat gave way to the cruel caricature of the Thousand-Year Reich.

A world view, then, is an all-inclusive conception which, when it is historically viable, integrates a group's imagery. According to our formula, it focuses disciplined attention on a selection of verifiable facts; it liberates a joint vision which enhances a sense of historical reality; and it actualizes a widening fellowship with strong work commitments. Altogether, these tendencies seem to confirm some historical truth previously only intuited. Please note the word "widening," however, because I believe that human evolution has a built-in tendency—spasmodically interrupted by periods of reactionary exclusion—to create wider identities toward an all-human consciousness.

In selecting a national vision for comparison with the structures of other products of human imagination, one is at first inclined to shy away from a phenomenon that has so expressly assumed the designation of a national "dream" and which, yet, has such a claim on the very essence of our daily experience. As to its origins and its persistence, we take the mythologist's word for it:

It is very probable that the behavior of the average American today, as well as the political and cultural ideology of the United States, still reflects the consequences of the Puritan certitude of having been called to restore the Earthly Paradise.[13]

The most outstanding aspect of the developing American Dream is its proven capacity, on the largest scale, to invite the most diverse people, motivated to come to this country for the most disparate reasons, to make a more inclusive vision out of the elements of many belief systems—and this in one or two generations. That this may yet have a prophetic potential for further unifications of the pseudo-species now extant both here and abroad—that, I believe, is attested to even by the despairing laments which I quoted at the start of this book. Those serious commentators would not indulge in such traumatized and repetitious descriptions of how the dream is turning into a nightmare did they not themselves believe in its original function and its potential survival value for persons as well as nations. A dream, however, must be completed: to awake in the middle of it—that *is* a nightmare. How this works in history is a question no single field of inquiry could claim to answer. But I can begin to review some aspects of our dream according to the dimensions of the ego space-time which we recognized at work in a child's play, in a young person's dream, and in other spheres of imagination. For a world view to be shared as both personally and communally relevant, its dimensions would have to permit the individual to associate the ego's means of creating inner orientation with the methods and images representative of a collective orientation—which is one strong reason for our personifying in language as well as in imagery as super-persons such entities as "the nation," "the church," or "the revolution."

This space-time must be grounded, I have said, in the ways in which any language combines in one perspective the "I" 's experience of what is faced in *front* and what is *ahead*, what is *in back* and lies *behind*—and then, what is *above* in front or in back and what is *below* in back or in front and how all these directions are alternately endowed with emotions of existential power: awe and dread, desire and anxiety, hope and fear, aggression and flight, love and rage. In all this, the "I" must remain the experiencing center with a sense of active choice as well as a sense of being chosen and sanctioned.

But to coordinate, rather than to set against each other, the conglomerate of "I"s that makes up a community—that is the task of shared visions, as so many ancient words connoting vision attest: Veda and Providence; history and ideology; individuality and indivisibility; viewpoint, evidence—and provision. A world view, therefore, must have compelling appeal for the most magic and universal hopes of the unconscious as well as the expectations fostered throughout childhood by daily ritualization; and it must be in accord with the letter and the spirit of institutional processes. Only thus will it yield time-bound power to arouse productive and communal energy in the greatest variety of individuals at a given moment in history.

It must be obvious that in the discussion of such a formidable phenomenon I can contribute only to the elucidation of the first criterion mentioned here, namely, the evidence of any world view's successful appeal to the largely unconscious needs of the individual ego space-time as accrued through childhood and youth; while, in pointing to some themes in the American Dream, I may unduly emphasize in what way this collective vision has acquired some qualities of a dream and some propensities for nightmare. This is what the representative commentators quoted at the beginning seemed to ask; wherefore some of the answers, too, may be in terms of the period we have all lived through.

I will take some initial leads from Robert Bellah's re-markable paper on a "public religious dimension expressed in a set of beliefs, symbols and rituals that I am calling the American civil religion." [14] Bellah borrowed this term from Rousseau's *Social Contract*, where it is defined as consisting of the elements of "the existence of God, the life to come, the reward of virtue and the punishment of vice, and the exclusion of religious intolerance." [15] He concentrates on the inauguration of American presidents "as an important ceremonial event in this religion. It reaffirms, among other things, the religious legitimation of the highest political authority." [16]

What Bellah describes, then, is some numinous aspect of the American vision as reaffirmed nowhere more profoundly than in the Gettysburg Address, and nowhere more pro-grammatically than by George Washington, who called this country "the experiment entrusted to the hands of the American people." [17] From that day on, our presidents, duly elected, forever inaugurated renewals of a world view which eventually came to bear names such as New Deal, New Frontier, or Great Society, thereby declaring the American people to have reelected themselves to improvise their own destiny.[18] Bellah points out an important and yet only seeming paradox: "although matters of personal re-ligious belief, worship, and association are considered to be strictly private affairs, there are, at the same time, certain common elements of religious orientation that the great majority of Americans share." [19] And, indeed, that ideal ambassador from the old world to the new, de Tocqueville, was already aware of not only the ceremonial but also the popular aspect of the civil religion: "They brought," he wrote, "with them into the new world a form of Christianity which I can not better describe than by styling it a democratic and republican religion." [20] As a truly native American writer, Melville, put it: "The political Messiah . . . has come in Us."

But who, then, is the corresponding new man and where the new leeway? What Washington called the experiment can be designated as the most extensive historical attempt to create on a continent reserved for it by providence a new national identity out of the identities of the colonists, settlers, and waves of immigrants coming from the nations and cultures of the world. It speaks for the power of vision of the founders (men as yet of a certain cultural and creedal uniformity) that they created a constitutional and cultural framework on the basis of which, even under unforeseen quantitative and qualitative diversity, a new man continued to be envisaged, a historical vulnerability perceived as pervasive strength, a prophecy confirmed. If this came to be called a "melting pot," with the connotation of a bubbling, powerful mixture, we should consider that this now so easy phrase also implies a warning of the danger of being melted beyond recognition, without any certainty that the conglomerate would result in a superior amalgamation marking a common future for all. The possible elimination of age-old identities thus added much emotional uncertainty to the unbelievable hardships endured by successive "first generations." The result was a polarization of some preserved ethnicity with a grandiose inter-ethnic solidarity—one polarization among many that make up the singularity of a nation's identity, as derived, as I put it years ago, "from the ways in which history has, as it were, counterpointed certain opposite potentialities; the ways in which it lifts this counterpoint to a unique style of civilization." [21]

The new type of man, of course, came to be called the "self-made" man, a personal and national self-image to be sustained on an open continent ready for vast and joint improvisation: and what a playground it proved to be—for many! (The play was eventually reflected in the humor: when one man boasted of being self-made, another called him a conspicuous example of the product of unskilled labor. And when someone in Congress called Andrew Johnson a self-made man, Thaddeus Stevens said he was glad to hear this because it relieved the Almighty of a tremendous responsibility.) And, indeed, there is more than a suggestion that the self-made man competes with the Maker Himself—or, at least, cooperates with Him. And do not men who make or remake themselves thereby implicitly deny their fathers' and mothers' fatherlands and mother countries; and may their hybris not burden them with a specific guilt to be borne—borne by different ethnic and religious groups, and by different individuals, in a variety of distinctive ways?

Arrival by the crossing of a body of water often carries the connotation of birth. Early America, in fact, identified with the people of Israel; for in order to arrive here in earnest and to feel sanctioned in the conquest of the new land, there had to be a divinely decreed exodus from the tyranny of some Egypt—and a crossing. This mythical recapitulation of a joint past bestowed on the various forms of exodus from the old countries an inspired voluntarism, while it transformed those who had to emigrate or wished to emigrate into a chosen people, and therefore guiltless and blameless of having deserted or having been driven away from a family, a country, a culture, or a language.

As for the scheme of everyday ritualization which we have found to be the very fabric of a culture, it is obvious that a work ethic is most central to every kind of "new man." In this country, a new ritualization of work roles emerged, emphasizing an essential equality of all who freely chose a chance to improve their status—on whatever level. From childhood on, inventive industry and playful initiative were cultivated, for what counted was to make things grow and to make things work. Where history, geography, and technology all reward such a joint sense of initiative with an ever expanding leeway and with growing prosperity (or the convincing promise of both), whatever guilt may be suggested by the idea of replacing the older generations seems forever assuaged by the chance of moving and growing away from the old folks—and this with their fervent encouragement—into new territory, new fields. To the arrival over the big water was added the trial of westward migration. Thus, the self-made way of life glorified its own type of man, who could ruthlessly grasp expansive opportunities and who was therefore granted the natural right to ignore or exploit those "types" not so inclined or not so favored by opportunities. Today, of course, one cannot recall the writings or review the paintings which tell of the time of the founders without marveling at the role (and official no-role) of women in it all, and how it came about that they not only could accept their assigned place as man's complement and adornment, but could devote to it the energy of life-givers and value bearers in home, school, and community.

It was to be called a "way of life"—a most restrained term as far as great nations go; for it must be said that, at least for the European contingent, the American way of life was a most radical experiment in overcoming the national and religious hates traditionally expressed and renewed in the old world in habitual periodical warfare between close neighbors. The best documented and the most celebrated aspect of the new world's independence from the old, namely, how the new way of life was personified and represented by its founders, who incorporated in the Constitution and the Bill of Rights the elemental concepts of life, liberty, and the pursuit of happiness—that, unfortunately, I cannot dwell on here. Let me emphasize only that the founders of the American system in their foresight set out to establish checks and balances which would permit not only variety to flourish within the confines of an elastic lawfulness, but also gamesmanship to manifest itself on a grand, if sometimes turbulent, arrangement of forces, as in the two-party system.

The American Dream has thus clearly fostered history's most promising attempt at the political containment of what we have described as man's most dangerous evolutionary burden, namely, his pseudo-speciation. Yet this human proclivity found its place—on the boundaries of the dream. At first, the combination of national independence and political revolution created a strong sense of having left both despotism and serfdom behind geographically and historically. Yet from the beginning the dream assigned a pseudo-mythic function to the Indians, who *were there* in that newly conquered "emptiness"; and it took for granted the segregation of the blacks, whose arrival on these shores was anything but self-chosen: to them, Egypt was *here* ("let my people go"). And if a "way of life" needs witches on whom to project diabolic intentions, America has had its "real" witches [22] from the beginning, and, later, a variety of "witch hunts." Justice does, indeed, tend to blind itself whenever a new and glorified man needs inferior countermen, as a bright foreground needs a dark background. Thus, any system is apt to create some dead ends; and the ritualistic aspects of a collective dream become most strident exactly where righteousness and prejudice collude with each other in the rationalized curtailment or confinement of some classes of human beings, whether they are banned to spheres of inactivation, or relegated to slave quarters, reservations, or ghettos. The American civil religion, of course, found its great moment of self-appraisal in Lincoln's Second Inaugural Address.

With the Civil War, a new theme of death, sacrifice, and rebirth enters the civil religion. It is symbolized in the life and death of Lincoln. Nowhere is it stated more vividly than in the Gettysburg Address, itself part of the Lincolnian "New Testament" among the civil scriptures. Robert Lowell has recently pointed out the "insistent use of birth images" in the speech explicitly devoted to "these honored dead": "Brought forth," "conceived," "created," "a new birth of freedom." [23]

Thus, the theme of perpetual rebirth emerged from the national nightmare of civil war.

Shared Nightmares

How THE American way of life, with its singular indus-triousness and amiability, its teamwork, precision, and rou-tinization, its special brand of courage and its inventive competitiveness, its playfulness and showmanship struck me as an immigrant and as a therapist and student of chil-dren I have recorded, here and there, in my earlier writ-ings. This ritualization of everyday life remains central to the future of the dream. To the counterpointed themes al-ready postulated, however, we must now add those of *communal closeness* and of *immeasurable bigness,* which has led (in our terms) to gigantic ritualisms. With the de-velopment not only of a national union but also of an em-pire marked by mercantile and industrial expansion, national politics and the civil religion combined (and colluded) in a variety of new deals which, under various names, reasserted an American creed of newness *and* bigness as basic elements in the national identity.

Let me return, however, to the suggestion that historical truth is based on what is factual in the sense of material verifiability; on what is perceived as genuinely compelling reality; and on what can be actualized by communal effort. The most factual basis of a national sense of unlimited leeway is, of course, its extension in space (its real estate) and the relation of its earthly resources to the safety of its borders. In all these respects, America has been uniquely fortunate and almost invincibly so. But a study of the American Dream in all these respects would have to include the specific traumata which will abruptly mark the limits of a vision's leeway. A trauma in individual life is a shocking experience of such suddenness and intensity that a person's habitual sense of "play" is temporarily put out of commission; and a state of traumatization may persist beyond the best temporary readjustment in the form of a more or less conscious expectation of the trauma's recurrence. An emphasis in one's way of life on newness and bigness invites two kinds of traumata: one marking a sudden halt to expansion, and one revealing an overexpansion which defeats adjustment. A sampling of historical traumatizations should introduce us to the nightmarish quality which the national dream assumed periodically and maintained, as it were, subliminally. In peacetime and in their daily lives, Americans lived in the hope that the colossal strivings and hardships now almost forgotten by affluent America had, indeed, bought safe and unlimited opportunities for those who continued to "better themselves." But the Great Depression demonstrated the limits to material initiative. And this country has always counted on an open, an "outer" space of great proportions: first in the "Wild West" and then also on foreign battlegrounds, where American armies always were *expeditionary* forces sent abroad in order to prevent any inimical ideological power from ever being in a position of invading this continent; and, we must remember, the men manning those expeditions were faced with invading some of those same "old countries" which had fathered and mothered their grandparents and even their parents. But the eventual advent of the nuclear age, while at first appearing to be gloriously in line with America's expansive dreams, made all borders, natural or fortified, obsolete.

With time, self-made America also became a model of technological know-how and world marketing. The export of what was "made in America" seemed to provide the dream with further overwhelming material confirmation such as was (who could doubt it?) also planned by a pragmatic providence. Free enterprise and reckless expansion did not need to apologize to those who felt exploited or left out or to the countryside which became polluted. Nor was it perceived as a new form of imperialism when, wherever American know-how spread, a new super-identity (of which the supermarket became a fitting symbol envied even by the "other side") came along in a package deal.

America's technological triumph reached its pinnacle in the televisit to the moon. One astronaut linked the old and the new game by bringing along his golf club. But it was all made somewhat vainglorious by a presidential voice which told mankind that this was the "greatest moment since creation" and that the astronauts were now seeing the earth "as God sees it." In the meantime, a new technical Way of Death, namely, the passionless use of overkill, had already reached a pinnacle in Hiroshima. But the country awakened only slowly to the fact that it had been chosen by fate to initiate the most modern version of what Loren Eiseley calls the "lethal element in the universe." In Alamogordo and Hiroshima (as well as on the moon), the dream somehow surpassed its own native comprehension. The triumph of power they revealed could not redeem the sense that modern life made all too many people aimless and voiceless robots in a blueprint without boundaries—a blueprint often adjusted not by any wisdom of comprehensive planning but by a continuous readjustment to inexorable changes without meaningful alternatives, permitting only ritualistic responses instead of a vitalizing re-ritualization.

Thus, the mere quantity of expansion and production which permitted the new man to enjoy what he had wrought gradually also put some severe stress on the quality of communal life; and the American combination of dreaming and scheming led to hyper-organization and over-standardization, vast bureaucratization and competitive professionalization. Masses of individuals, having learned to "make like" free men and hoping for the chance to make something of themselves, were instead confirmed in stereotyped roles within the politics of narrow and confining conditions. We also know how the over-all vision of an unimpaired individualism contained in and maintained by the consent of the governed led, in the explosive increase of mere quantities of people and goods, to a complexity in legislation and law enforcement in which many an individual (unless he happened to know how to play a corner of the power game) soon lost the sense of fair play, or (for that matter) of any play at all. And I need not repeat that

the loss of playful leeway, especially if to be free and playful is the stance one lives by, results in a certain sense of
stagnation. Yet the majority would not and could not envisage radical change; for had not the original vision been
based on a revolutionary new man who might yet appear in
truer form to save us and the world?

And then there was the Vietnam war, seemingly just another highway of colonial politics but gradually ending in
a dead-end road such as was bemourned by the chorus of
commentators quoted at the beginning. A new sense of
reality obviously needed humanist sources of outrage to
counteract the new and pervasive conviction of the good-
ness of mechanized destruction and of the objectivity and
the moral neutrality, if not superiority, of him who wields it.
For this brand of "technicism," to use Robert Lifton's term,
has since the battle of the Somme and World War II's satu-
ration bombing acquired a weapon (now in the hands of
others, too) which could end mankind's major gains. At
any rate, this country eventually found itself committed
to a war so expensive and so over-mechanized and yet so
all-round hopeless that no victory, no liberation, but only
an extrication "without dishonor" was left as an immediate
national goal. Yet, the dream did survive even this event
without major panic or without an overwhelming sense of
having been checkmated in its vision. But just then Watergate offered itself as a radically new focus of concern over
the "irrealities" which had been permitted to take over the
nation at the top.

What I have been able to sketch of this country's origins
has amply illustrated, I hope, what I have claimed a shared
new vision can provide for all (or most) who partake in it:

a sense of centrality and of choice, of awareness and orientation, and of superior efficacy. But if I would now look for a simple example of clinical historicity as a counterpart to those despairing voices of erudite comment, I submit that it would take only a few quotations from that original journalistic piece which brought the massacre of My Lai to the world's attention to illustrate the total loss of military ritualization on the part of some of our young men; and their prevailing sense of being on a lost periphery, of being inactivated, confounded, and overwhelmed—and, therefore, filled with a rage without any familiar pattern. In this one event (as, indeed, in much of this war), we did let our soldiers indeed become the victims of a nightmare in broad daylight.

One must read Seymour Hersh's masterly account [24] of that day when a company of eighteen- to twenty-two-year-old Americans, half of them black and half white, were dropped on a faraway hamlet in what was to be their first action against an enemy most had never seen, in order to destroy the village which was supposed to be his stronghold. To the captain, it had looked like a tough fight. He had expected his men to be outnumbered at least two to one, but he had faith in the firepower of his infantrymen, and of the helicopter and gun-ship crews. By then, of course, the communist counter-ritualization of guerrilla tactics had undermined much confidence in the logistics and professionalism of traditional and technological warfare; for it became the rule that one got "hit from the rear." And the captain had spoken of revenge and had exhorted his men to see to it that "nothing would be walking, growing, or crawling," and, in fact, "nothing would be living" when they were through. Their own conflicting orders, one soldier said later, "could be interpreted in different ways by different persons according to their emotional structure"— exactly what an order should *not* be. And, indeed, what did happen also reveals in absurd condensation the violent symptoms of an acute de-ritualization of the military training which, in this engagement, was to be baptized by the fire of combat.

The scenario, as seen from above—that is, from the lofty clouds in which the commanding planes were circling and from the desks of the faraway strategists—looked well planned: the air lanes were carefully allotted to high-ranking officers, the commanding general hovering at two thousand feet, the lower-flying door gunners spraying protective fire. The first platoon came firing out of the landed craft while other companies blocked escape routes to prevent the VC troops from fleeing. Only there *was* no visible enemy, and no resistance to speak of. The men could not see thirty feet from the landing zone, and the various groups could not see each other. And since the enemy seemed to be everywhere and nowhere, "they were all psyched up," "it was almost a chain reaction," they were "no longer burdened by questions of differentiation," "everything became a target," and "they were giving in to an easy pattern of violence."

Some men began to feel as if not enemy soldiers but crawling creatures were surrounding them and, soon, as if "cockroaches were all over you." Thus, the most unsoldierly of all orders—to kill "anything old enough to walk"— seemed to fit the image of vermin threatening to overrun them. The lieutenant (about whom one of his men said that he reminded him of a "kid trying to play war" and "to make something out of himself he wasn't") had said, "Waste them." What followed nobody could observe in its entirety, but four hundred and fifty to five hundred people were mowed down: as the official report specifies, "oriental human beings, occupants of the village of My Lai 4, whose names and sexes [the report did not dare to add "and ages"] are unknown."

And, indeed, it seems that one prime result of catastrophic de-ritualization throughout history is the loss of the instinctual impulse to spare children.

The last statement quoted by Hersh, "The people didn't know what they were dying for and the guys didn't know why they were shooting them," [25] contains the whole story, if one will only attend to the implications of each word.

There were, of course, outstanding and unforgettable instances when men spared and saved whom they could.

What could be the use, the reader may ask, so close to the end of a book, to introduce a last illustration which, to many, may not seem to be more than a freak occurrence or, at the most, typical of a number of accidents unavoidable in warfare? I have referred to the story as an example of that deadliness which takes over when all gamesmanship has gone out of an adult scenario. For this was not old-fashioned war as may be depicted, say, in Goya's cruel etchings, nor a holocaust committed by fanatic storm troopers. Their own words reveal some of our soldiers as being beyond such historical patterns and as sensitive to the betrayal of their over-all identity as soldiers and as Americans. It would be a sad service to the Dream to simply forget such nightmares.

And we owe it to the children who provide us with toy configurations to indicate the whole range of scenarios which must be seen as related when matters of ritualization and de-ritualization are applied to crises of national proportions. In sketching the American Dream and claiming its persistence through history, we cannot bypass the fact that this country, too, has stepped into the center of the existential dilemma which other empires have had to confront in history. And even as this country's history has been so self-consciously self-chosen, it also seems to be prepared by its proven patterns of renewal to acknowledge some ends-of-the-road of national and technological expansion not as a defeat but as a conscious step toward making the American vision universally relevant.

Visions and Countervisions

In an emerging world view, we have attempted to recognize the most powerful adult version of that scenario of a mastered leeway which we saw, stage for stage, in the development of playful imagination. We have also suggested that such playfulness, throughout ontogeny, is placed in the service both of an inner ordering of experience and of the ritualizations of everyday life which introduce the growing individual into functioning institutions. It is this coherent character, so intangible and yet compelling and convincing when it works, which confirms and sanctions a vocabulary and an imagery pervading both the stages of human growth and the basic elements of all social order. If I should point once more to some parallels in all shared visions while reminding us of the play construction, of the dream, and of the Vision on the Wall, I would say that in the center is the image of a new human type created by elemental natural or historical events and emerging at a chosen moment in a chosen place to represent a wider, more inclusive identity unifying previously separate and, in fact, suppressed identities. This new image is consonant with new techniques of production (including weapons) and methods of factual verification, and thus with the availability of new natural and social resources of energy. The new type is in possession of a vocabulary and an imagery through which the voices of the deity or of ancestors, of prophets or founders, of seers or thinkers, can be perceived to make inspiring sense ready to liberate those who can hear, while all false prophets appear exposed, and their believers are marked as expendable. A new historical mythology shows how early traumatic hardships have been miraculously managed, a certain doom has been averted, and thus early usurpations have proven justified; while the new conditions, if carefully watched and guarded in their legal and political indivisibility, can forever assure a chosen state of unlimited potentials. This seems to guarantee a transcendent identity, a kind of collective immortality outwitting any imaginable apocalypse, and the accidents and disasters of death. Evil, on the other hand, is always reincarnated in the inner world as the new negative identity which is the shadow of the new positive one; and in the outer world in that corresponding other-species which, if it cannot be kept in its place, must be destroyed.

In any given world view, one or the other of these constituent elements may manifest itself most variably; and there is an overwhelming literature, from mythology to historiography, which collects, transmits, and analyzes the variety of the more formalized and more ritual versions.

In speaking of a "way of life," however, we are interested to learn of the ways in which a world view professedly or tacitly reaches into the minds and motivations of the participants. It may be explicit and effusive on ceremonial occasions and yet almost hidden in the ritualizations of daily life—and hidden precisely because it is taken for granted. Some of its fundamentals thus have a commanding place in everybody's, the dissenters' as well as the loyalists', configurations of speech and thought, and this especially when historical upheavals may force decisively new connotations on them. In fact, so we must emphasize in conclusion, all the dimensions outlined here so schematically as making up one world view can remain dynamically relevant only in a continuous and continuously surprising interplay of visions and countervisions which keeps alive certain basic antitheses. Of the dialectics involved in this process we have touched on those of the individual life cycle and the generational cycle; that of creative ritualization and ritualistic rigidity; and that of pseudo-speciation and common specieshood— while throughout a most basic dialectic was implied, namely, that of conscious and unconscious motivation.

This country has been, throughout her recent crises (as many times before), the scene of the most astonishing range of fragmentary countervisions, from the most militantly political and outspokenly critical to the most devotedly communal and quietly meditative: and it can well be reiterated that they all have manifested some form of sincere playfulness. True, we have seen how a number of countervisions, while making some unforgettable points, lose play and momentum from the mere strenuousness of being counter. The fact is that countervisions (whether they concern a new and beautiful blackness, a new and less compliant youth, or a new self-determined woman) often obsessively repeat, by simply reversing rather than transcending them, the already overly ritualistic categories of the existing order, whose imagery sometimes is so much better circumscribed than the counter-imagery suggested. A new moralism, however, often convinces only those who share a certain rage over having been oppressed by (and often also over having colluded with) the old moralism—a rage often dominant in the first stages of countervisions and yet necessary to make a point. At any rate, it does seem that, beyond the political goals reached or envisaged, a transformation reviving some traditional values of freedom within a more universal world view is discernible in the relations of the sexes; in education and community relations; in the attention to nutrition and the whole body; in a new respect for the person—of any age; and in ecological attitudes toward the environment as well as ecumenical ones toward spiritual matters. While often clannish and faddish, these trends nevertheless betray the emergence of a set of countervisions which, above all, are intended to counteract the exclusive dominance of technocracy in a more universal man.

But, as Bellah reminds us, even as revolutions must find their constitutions, so conversions must lead to covenants—and a countervision can prove the power of its covenant only by entering convincingly, if ever so upsettingly, into the ritualizations of everyday life.

In conclusion, let me return to my field, psychoanalysis, which emerged as a countervision in this century in the form of clinical enlightenment. In some significant ways, it was conceived and must be considered to be a countervision in perpetuity, for it insists that the observable facts of our existence include the workings of a dynamic unconscious, and that there is no reality and no actuality which is not codetermined by conflicting motivations which either enhance personal and communal leeway or must be understood in their destructiveness. This countervision has joined a number of established visions such as the medical and scientific ones. Incidentally, one suspects that it has found this country more hospitable than any other, not only because of the influence of some psychiatric pioneers, but also because in our metropolitan milieu it served as a restorative method of analyzing the leftovers of old orthodoxies and of alleviating the guilt over their abandonment, while helping to create a new "orthodox" and a host of "new-" and "post-Freudian" ritualizations in everyday life and language. On the other hand, psychoanalysis will, by its very nature, continue to be resisted everywhere in its perpetual mission, namely, the study of unconscious forces as they continue to reveal themselves in ongoing clinical observation and in changing theoretical concerns, both of which demand the self-observation of the observer from his relative place in changing history. This includes the study of the way in which different observers are influenced by or are oblivious to varying visions; and how what impresses one observer in a given field or country (or segments thereof) as the life-and-death struggle of a vital vision may be perceived by an observer in another country or circle as no more than a curious idiosyncrasy or aberration.

But I would suggest that it is in academic discussion that we should be given a chance to experiment with awareness, and to develop a certain informed relativism. For there is something in the nature of all shared visions which calls for transcendence by insight as we approach a more universal image of humanity. That the unconscious yields some of its nature to a widening consciousness may itself be part of an evolutionary happening. At the same time, the development of science and technology has radically altered the nature and the relative proportion of verifiable fact, shared reality, and imperative actuality in any emerging world view. The mystery and the burden of living in a present marked by an unthought-of leeway of manipulatory power, constructive and destructive, demand concentration on the verifiable as the core of man's dominant revelation and leeway, according to old man Einstein's reasons. Mankind cannot afford to propagate a variety of new consciousnesses without considering what we have begun to learn about the unconscious.

The psychoanalytic approach to historical relativity, by the same token, is not merely an "application" to historical actors or events of a completed psychological theory; it demands, rather, a certain continuing awareness of the function of changing theory in changing history. Our countervision has for long concentrated on the "inner economy" of individual human beings; but we have been confronted with the ecology governing the emergence of human energies through the stages of the life cycle as lived in social institutions. Any application of psychoanalysis to politics, be it the "politics" of everyday life or big politics, must take into consideration the generational and evolutionary dialectics involved.

Our work thus faces us with a dilemma shared in some form by all "countervisions in perpetuity" (such as religion, philosophy, and science), namely, the ambiguous interrelation of detached and yet empathic observation, theoretical clarity, healing intervention, and ideological participation. As one who has shared in the treatment and in the study of children, youths, and adults during decades of rapid changes in historical perspective, I have had to face the often perplexing *dialectics of social stability and social change* in their relative effect on the stages of life. There is always the central fact that society's renewal depends on the way in which a significant number of its *children* partake of a certain stability of basic ritualizations; its *young people* experience convincing confirmations or can find meaningful patterns of dissent or revolt; and its *adults* can participate in a given or an emerging system of political choices between conservation and innovation in productive and generational processes.

If the survival of essential childhood potentials, including the virtues of playfulness, depends on a certain stability in the ritualization of the process of growing up, then it is of special importance to clarify the relative contributions of men and women to such stability in past history, and to consider the way in which these contributions may now be enhanced by well-considered sharing. A child cannot develop a strong as well as adaptable and workable conscience —with playfulness to spare—without being guided by adults with a reasonably convincing consensus of ethical values within workable institutions. But neither can these institutions maintain their convincing function—and their elasticity—without a continuing feedback from the newcomers emerging through the generational process: a feedback which supports the established social *form* if it, indeed, continues to facilitate the interplay of inner and outer structure, or which insists on a reassertion of the *spirit* where it has fallen victim to an overgrown ritualism with the resulting alternations of license and bad conscience, undue leniency

and severity, anarchic drivenness and compulsive formalization.

If youth, furthermore, is the crucible where the strengths
and patterns of mutuality learned by ritualization in childhood encounter the society's role system, it is important to
study the conditions which would permit innovative playfulness and experimental passion to survive in the social
order. And if, finally, in adulthood an ethical orientation is
mandatory, then it is exactly the maintenance of the future
in terms of the informed attention given to the generational
process which through the advent of psychoanalysis has
become a more conscious mandate.

As to daily work, clinical psychoanalytic observation can
throw rare light on the way in which shared visions—
whether they appear as belief, conviction, or opinion, fantasy or illusion—are part of an individual's functioning, in
that they either encourage a certain actualization of trained
energies in interplay with communal and environmental
resources, or, indeed, impart a sense of being inactivated
and devitalized in an incomprehensible world. What happens, then, to an individual's inner life at any given stage
in the life history is always significantly related to the crises
of the social institutions predominant in the developing
world view at that historical moment. At any rate, it is
here that the psychoanalytic assessment of political reality
begins. For only when we are thus aware of the communal
core on which man's adaptation depends can we proceed to
recognize that combination of inner defenses and political
deals which is inherent in the distribution of power and
which ever again threatens all individuality and communality through ossification in legalistic, bureaucratic, and
technicist systems—the communal counterparts to individual

"defense mechanisms." If it has been a contribution of psychoanalysis to demonstrate, in history as well as in life histories, how the fixation on the past can hinder the anticipation of the future, undermining serious playfulness and emotional vitality, it may well prove of help in studies of how a given world view fulfills its mission, namely, to facilitate an optimal interplay of life cycles and institutions. But this means, at this stage of the game, the endeavor to integrate, on the smallest as well as the largest scale, the gigantic range of new facts mastered; to comprehend responsibly the transcendent reality of the American experience within a more inclusive human identity; and to help actualize daily life on the basis of what we are beginning to know of the nature of things—and of human nature.

Psychoanalysis could not contribute to such comparative work if it were not grounded in a deep belief in the power of Eros to imbue intimacy and communality, work, worship, and awareness with a measure of true play. In this sense, let me come back to Plato's suggestion that the leap is the model of playfulness, and let me wish us all great leaps—and firm landings.

Notes

Notes

PREFACE
(*pages* 11–12)

1. Maria W. Piers, ed., *Play and Development: A Symposium* (New York: Norton, 1972).

2. Sir Julian Huxley, ed., "A Discussion on Ritualisation of Behaviour in Animals and Men," in *Philosophical Transactions of the Royal Society of London*, ser. B, no. 772, vol. 251 (1966), pp. 247–526.

3. *Dimensions of a New Identity: The 1973 Jefferson Lectures in the Humanities* (New York: Norton, 1974).

I. PLAY AND VISION
(*pages* 19–60)

1. All this and what follows was noted in 1972. As I ready the book for print, a curtain has come down over Vietnam and another has opened and closed on the home-town spectacle of Watergate; and the nightmare has been declared over by a new president. The curtain also closed over a president's tenure, about whom a former president (Truman) had said decades ago that he was one of the few people he knew who *really* did not know whether he was telling the truth or was lying. Nevertheless, the now ex-president had been elected by a landslide, called "unreal" by some commentators at the time; and up to the last day he had worked

stubbornly on the historical image he was determined to leave behind, saving the very tapes which then incriminated him.

2. Walter Kerr, *New York Times.*

3. Hannah Arendt, "Lying in Politics: Reflections on the Pentagon Papers," *New York Review of Books,* Nov. 18, 1971, p. 30.

4. *Ibid.,* p. 33.

5. *Ibid.,* quoted from Pentagon Papers, pp. 436, 438.

6. *Ibid.,* p. 30.

7. Tom Wicker, *New York Times,* April 20, 1972.

8. George W. Ball, "The Trap of Rationality," *Newsweek,* July 26, 1971, p. 64.

9. *Ibid.*

10. John K. Fairbank, *New York Review of Books,* Feb. 24, 1972.

11. Compare the trip up the Nile of the same president, greeted with organized enthusiasm by Egyptian peasants, while a majority of his own people began to refuse him the most ordinary credibility.

12. John Leonard, "The Last Word: Show Biz and Serious Biz," *New York Times,* Dec. 19, 1971.

13. *Time,* May 17, 1971.

14. J. M. McLuhan, Note on the First Meeting, *Delos Symposium (Delos 10),* Athens Center of Ekistics, Document B, no. 21, July 11, 1972.

15. Walter Lippmann, *Public Opinion* (New York: Macmillan, 1922; paperback ed., 1960), p. 30.

16. *Ibid.,* p. 27.

17. *Ibid.,* p. 28.

18. *Ibid.,* pp. 15–16.

19. *Ibid.,* p. 27.

20. Yet, just before Watergate broke, I happened to meet one of President Nixon's closest advisers. A decidedly pragmatic man, he asked, "I hear, Professor, that you spent the day in the Senate. What was your impression?" "Unreal," I said, "in the midst of the most frightening realities." "You should come to the White House!" he exclaimed.

21. L. N. J. Kamp and E. S. Kessler, "The World Test," *Journal of Child Psychology and Psychiatry,* vol. 2 (1970), pp. 81–108.

22. Piers, ed., *Play and Development,* pp. 128–30.

23. *Ibid.,* p. 27.

24. For the method employed, see *Childhood and Society* (New York: Norton, 1950; 2nd ed., 1963), pp. 97–108.

25. J. Huizinga, *Homo Ludens: A Study of the Play-Element in Culture* (London: Routledge and Kegan Paul, 1949), p. 10.

26. *Ibid.*

27. Piers, ed., *Play and Development,* pp. 43–63.

28. *Ibid.,* p. 54.

29. Joan Erikson, "Eye to Eye," in Gyorgy Kepes, ed., *The Man-Made Object* (New York: Braziller, 1966).

30. J. S. Bruner, *Processes of Cognitive Growth: Infancy* (Worcester, Mass.: Clark University Press, 1968), p. 7.

31. *Ibid.,* p. 8.

32. *Ibid.,* p. 32.

33. Jean Piaget, *Construction of Reality in the Child* (New York: Basic Books, 1954), p. 3.

34. Lloyd de Mause, ed., *The History of Childhood* (New York: Psychohistory Press, 1974, p. 1.

35. Gerald Holton, "Mach, Einstein, and the Search for Reality," *Daedalus*, vol. 97, no. 2 (1967), pp. 636–73.

II. LIFE CYCLE AND RITUALIZATION
(*pages 70–117*)

1. Brian Sutton-Smith, "The Game as a School of Abstraction," in Loyda M. Shears and Eli M. Bower, eds., *Games in Education and Development* (Springfield, Ill.: C. C. Thomas, 1974).

2. Iranaus Eibl-Eibesfeldt, "Concepts of Ethology and Their Significance in the Study of Human Behavior," in H. W. Stevenson et al., *Early Behavior* (New York: Wiley, 1967), pp. 127–46.

3. E. H. Erikson, *Gandhi's Truth* (New York: Norton, 1969).

4. What follows has first been reported in Huxley, "A Discussion on Ritualisation of Behaviour in Animals and Men." See also K. Lorenz's corresponding report, *Philosophical Transactions of the Royal Society* (1966), pp. 278–84.

5. *Childhood and Society*, p. 177.

6. In a fascinating contribution to the symposium on ritualization in which I first enlarged on these ideas, R. D. Laing characterized some psychotic behavior (such as that of a prospective patient who invited him for lunch but neglected to feed him and then asked for his professional help) as a "de-ritualization of normal human rituals" according to a "privately elaborated code." He interpreted this "as a self-invalidating by invalidating the ritual of validation." As could be expected, he also had some questions concerning the ritual of giving papers in the Royal Society. (See *Philosophical Transactions of the Royal Society* (1966), pp. 331–36.)

7. Technically speaking, I would suggest that both the changing symptomatology and the inner defenses observed in clinical work can be seen to be related to changes in a society's patterns of ritualization. There appear to be direct correspondences between the genetic classifications of symptoms (compulsive or hysteric, say) and the ritualism described above (such as legalism or impersonation)—so much so that mental diseases can, indeed, be seen as private ritualisms.

III. SHARED VISIONS
(*pages 122–164*)

1. *Boston University Journal*, vol. 20 (Autumn, 1972), pp. 16–21.

2. Bertram Lewin, *The Image and the Past* (New York: International Universities Press, 1968).

3. *Ibid.*, pp. 21, 22.

4. Sigmund Freud, "Constructions in Analysis," Standard Edition of

the *Complete Psychological Works* (London: Hogarth Press, 1953; New York: Norton, 1976), vol. 23, p. 268.

5. Roy Schafer, "The Psychoanalytic Vision of Reality," *International Journal of Psycho-Analysis,* vol. 51, part 3 (1970), p. 279.

6. *Ibid.,* p. 289.

7. Gerald Holton,*Thematic Origins of Scientific Thought* (Cambridge, Mass.: Harvard University Press, 1973), p. 359.

8. *Ibid.,* p. 368.

9. *Ibid.,* pp. 368–69.

10. Albert Einstein, "Autobiographical Notes," in Paul A. Schilpp, ed., *Einstein: Philosopher Scientist* (New York: Harper Torchbooks, 1973), vol. 1, p. 7.

11. Holton, p. 377.

12. *Ibid.*

13. Mircea Eliade, *The Quest* (Chicago: University of Chicago Press, 1969), p. 99.

14. Robert N. Bellah, "Civil Religion in America," *Daedalus* (Winter, 1967), p. 4.

15. *Ibid.,* p. 5.

16. *Ibid.,* p. 4.

17. *Ibid.,* p. 7.

18. *Ibid.,* p. 3.

19. *Ibid.,* p. 13.

20. E. L. Tuveson, *Redeemer Nation* (Chicago: University of Chicago Press, 1968), pp. 156–57.

21. *Childhood and Society,* p. 244.

22. Kai T. Erikson, *Wayward Puritans: A Study in the Sociology of Deviance* (New York: Wiley, 1966).

23. Bellah, "Civil Religion," p. 10.

24. Seymour Hersh, "My Lai 4," *Harper's,* May, 1970, pp. 53–84.

25. *Ibid.,* p. 84.